A TIME T
DECEIVE
By Sam Burnell

Sam Burnell

Please note, this book is written in British English, so some spellings will vary from US English.

For

Ian Burnell

The best Dad and a true inspiration

This book has travelled! It was written in the North East of England, York, Malta & Athens.

Contents

Introduction

Marnie Dobbes cursed Eldrich Slouch. She'd done everything he asked, and more, and then when it was time for her to leave, he'd wanted extra wood chopping, and bringing in from the yard.

Marnie had worked for Slouch just over three months and deeply regretted her decision. Before this, she'd worked as a buttoner for Master Argent on Needle Street. Argent had recommended her to the aged Slouch, and the offer of work as his private servant with an increase in her weekly pay and a room of her own at the back of his house had seemed like a gift from the Lord.

At first glance, Eldridge Slouch looked nothing other than an aged gentleman. Stooped-backed, with a silver-topped stick in his gnarled right hand that he leaned heavily upon. His clothes were fine and well-tailored, and his boots polished and made from supple leather. Slouch's head was always topped with a velvet, feather and fur-trimmed hat, defending what few threads of hair remained. Age had twisted his mouth, the right side drooped a little, the middle rose towards his nose, and the left puckered his cheek. It gave him the appearance of having a perpetually amused and amicable disposition. Marnie had found out very quickly that the seemingly smiling mouth never parted with kind words. After two weeks her delight in her new position had been seriously blighted.

Slouch felt he owned every hour she had. The only time he did not have tasks for her or demand her attendance was when he was asleep, and that, regretfully, wasn't long enough. And worse, if he had no use for her during the day, he'd send her to work in his botchers shop. Peggy Delwyn oversaw it for him, and had no liking for her at all. Marnie would invariably end up working outside, pounding rags in the troughs in a mixture of ashes and piss.

The troughs stank.

The spatter turned her skin red and the fumes made her eyes stream, to the point where she was almost thankful when Slouch demanded her presence again.

After the bells tolled for Vespers, he'd retire and take a meal in his room brought to him by Marnie. She'd wait then for the sound of his stick striking the wooden floor and return to collect the platters, refill his cup, stoke the fire, or if she was lucky light one in his room which meant he would be retiring soon. He rose early, before the bells struck for Prime, and he would have a list of tasks for her ready. Work would stretch out endlessly until Slouch finally took himself off to bed, a bed Marnie had warmed for him with a brick wrapped in lambs fleece. His bed was the largest piece of furniture in the house, there were initials carved into the foot board, Marnie knew them to be letters and assumed they related to Slouch and his long dead wife.

Slouch had announced he was retiring. Marnie took the brick from his bed, it was still blissfully warm. She'd put it into the bottom of her own bed and wrap her feet around it. If Slouch knew he'd be furious, but he wasn't likely to find out. Slouch, finished with the day, passed her on the stairs, she bobbed a half curtsey, one hand grasped her skirt hem, the other the fleece-wrapped brick, and she set her feet quickly in the direction of her own room.

Finally, her day was done.

"Before you finish, there's a package to collect from Finney's. Bring it to me in my room," Slouch barked down the stairs.

"At this time?" Marnie blurted before she could stop herself.

Slouch descended two steps towards her. "Insolent wench."

Before she could take another step backwards, the old man's hand connected with her ear, knocking her cap askew and producing a painful yelp from Marnie. "Get, ye gone, woman!"

Tears sprang to her eyes and gathered along her lower lids. Supressing a sob that came more from exhaustion than the scolding. Marnie retreated, bobbing something akin to a curtsey she left the wool wrapped brick on the hall floor and bolted for the door that led to the street.

Finney's wasn't far, two streets away. It was dark now, prematurely so. A sullen cloudy sky had ruined the June day stealing the sun. It was setting now, out of sight, hidden behind the buildings of the city. The faltering evening light lit the middle of the street, leaving the sides in darkness. The streets were already quiet, the shops had closed their shutters and doors, and trade was finished. There was little to tell of their existence apart from a pond of blood before Onop's butcher's shop and a flurry of curled shavings caught in the streets mud from Cady's the carpenters.

Finney's was at the end of the street, turn left, then turn left again and it was half-way along. Marnie paused for a moment just after Cady's shop, there was Cooper's alley that ran towards the street she needed. It was drenched in darkness, it was a shorter route, but not safe. Not only would she be unaware of anyone lurking in the darkness, the bottom of the alley was full of rubbish laying wait to snare her feet. You could navigate it during the day, but at night it was another matter. Grumbling, Marnie forced her tired legs to move her towards the end of the street, well aware that if she did not hurry, her nights slumber would be short.

She needed to find the time to change her employer. It was difficult when she had little opportunity to leave Slouch's house and even less time to talk to anyone. Maybe Finney's had work? She could at least ask?

Finney ran an apothecary's shop on Clough Street; it was his habit to take requests during the day, prepare the elixirs for his clients, and then make them available for collection in the evening. She had no idea what Slouch bought, but she had been three times already to collect an earthenware pot, neatly capped with linen and tied with a tight cord. A faint and sickly scent seeped through the cloth, but Marnie had no idea what was inside and no desire to know.

Arriving at the apothecaries, Marnie stepped inside the warm interior, instantly enveloped in the smell of herbs and spices. It was an earthy aroma, not at all unpleasant, and it reminded her of summer when the banks of the river were in bloom with cow parsley and foxgloves. From every beam in the shop hung tightly tied dried bunches of herbs. Four beams were given over to rosemary and rue, the rest held lines of parsley, sage, fennel, feverfew and elder, the wood showing through from the roof where bunches had been plucked for use.

Finney recognised her now and smiled. He was at least friendly.

"You've come for Master Slouch," he said, smiling. Turning, he retrieved a pot she now recognised from the shelf and held it out. "Take this for him and be sure to tell him to get in touch. I fear he is using more than he should."

Marnie bobbed a quick curtsey, muttered an acceptance of his words, took the pot and made her way quickly from the shop, cursing herself for not having the nerve to ask about work. Time was limited, and she wanted to go to bed. With her shawl pulled tightly around her shoulders, and the pot held tightly in both hands, Marnie made her way back towards Slouch's house as quickly as she could. Her determined march hesitated as she neared Cady's shop, and the darkened alley beckoned her.

She changed her direction and neared the entrance to the alley. If she took it, she would return to Slouch's house in half the time. Marnie stared into the darkness. Nothing. All that came back to her was complete silence.

"Stop being a prattling fool!" she said out-loud, straightening her shoulders Marnie stepped towards the oblong of blackness that was Cooper's alley.

The alley bent half-way along, after that she'd be able to see the light from the exit. It wasn't far to the middle. Holding the pot tightly she stepped carefully into the narrow passage, placing each wooden shoe down with care on the uneven surface. The alley was open to the sky above, but the building on the right, Inston's leather shop, overhung it and so for the first half of her journey there wasn't even any light from above at all.

Half-way towards the bend Marnie was enveloped in the pitch black. Clutching the jar protectively to her chest she kept going.

The cloth on her right shoulder snagged, and something grabbed at her arm.

Marnie yelped.

She tripped, lost her balance, and cannoned into the wall to her right; releasing one hand from its hold on the pot, she flung it out to save herself. Her palm slapped hard against rough timber, driving a dozen splinters into her skin. Tears, unwanted, sprang to her already reddened eyes. Marnie let out a sob, sniffed loudly and brushed the back of her hand against her wet eyes. She'd stumbled blindly into a stack of rough-cut wood propped against the wall at the side of Inston's workshop.

Marnie sniffed hard again, navigated back to where she thought the middle of the passage was and set her feet towards the bend where the light would reveal her exit. It seemed further than it should have been, all before her was still the unending blackness of the alley.

Something unseen and angular was beneath her right foot when she put it down. The wooden shoe slid down the side of the object, and her weight shifted over it, painfully twisting her ankle.

Marnie sobbed again. Tears of self-pity dripped from her cheeks, and she limped down the narrow alley gripping the pot in shaking hands.

Ahead of her, a grey slit in the dark began to appear, and Marnie let out a long and relieved breath. It was the middle, the grey the herald of the light that was seeping in after the bend in the alley. Limping a little quicker, she reached it and turned down into the dim light of the remaining alley. She paused and wiped her clammy palms on her apron, and swept a strand of hair away from her eyes with a shaking hand.

She could now see the traps laid out for her in the gloom and avoid them. A broken barrel stave, a large block of decaying wattle and a tangle of rotten rope could be avoided. Despite the pain in her ankle, she made it to the end and back into the comparatively light street quickly. Not long now, and she would be at Slouch's. Not long now, and she'd be in bed. All she had to do was deliver the reeking pot to Slouch, and that was it. Her night was over.

Stomping along the street, she arrived shortly at the front of Slouch's botchers shop. The entrance to his house was through the workshop. The outer door wasn't locked, once inside a door on the left, latched on the inside, led to the botchers shop, and in front of her was Slouch's door. Opening it, she entered, the dim glow of an oil lamp on a side shelf illuminating the stairs. Closing the door behind her she dropped the latch into place securing the door.

Slouch's room was on the top floor. She didn't really want to take the pot up to him. When she had fetched it for him before, he had been seated downstairs before the fire. Marnie resolved to take the pot up, knock on his door, and leave it outside for him. That would be quick, and then she would be downstairs in the room she slept in behind the kitchen, finally able to slip her aching feet from her shoes and close her eyes on the day.

The wooden stairs went three-quarters of the way to the next floor and then turned abruptly to the left. Marnie was nearly at the top when she heard voices, one of which she recognised. Marnie relaxed immediately. At least Slouch wasn't alone. He tended to keep his temper under control when there were others around. She'd just put the pot outside the door, call quickly to say it was there, and then leave.

Marnie rounded the bend in the stairs, and her plan shattered like winter ice. Her feet took her automatically up one more step, where she stopped dead, staring into Eldridge Slouch's bed chamber.

All she could see of the old man were his arms; the sleeves of the bedgown had slipped away, and they wheeled frantically above his head, pale and clad with slack flesh. The fingers clawed and plucked at the pillow that was obscuring his face. His feet jostled beneath the bed covers, the legs convulsing. There was so very little noise, a muffled low moan, although she wasn't sure if she imagined it and the soft sound of Eldridge's feet as they kicked and spasmed beneath the covers.

Marnie dropping the pot, turned and bolted. Taking the stairs two at a time, her legs threatening to buckle beneath her. Landing heavily on the last step the weakened ankle gave way, her shoe flew from her foot and Marnie landed in a heap at the foot of the stairs. Scrabbling, on her hands and knees, she propelled herself towards the door, throwing her hands against it.

Latched, it held fast.

A desperate cry escaped from her throat. Scrambling her way up the door, she pushed the latch from the iron holder, and her fingers wrapped around the edge of the heavy door, hauling it open. She'd got it part-way open when it was slammed shut. Marnie felt the weight of her pursuer against her back; their foul breath caressing her cheek, and the door closed with her fingers trapped in the jam.

Marnie howled in agony as flesh and bone were crushed and bent around the angular frame.

"Hush girl!" The words delivered another gust of reeking breath to her nose.

"Please ...." Marnie begged, her voice high-pitched.

A cackle of amused laughter echoed in her ear.

"Please," her plea was weaker, quieter, and the pain in her fingers was subsiding.

"Another moment, girl, and you'll have your peace," the voice said. Then there was something else, another voice, further away, but Marnie didn't recognise her own screams as she slipped into a blackness darker than that of Cooper's alley.

Chapter 1

If asked what his calling was, Myles Devereux might smirk and call himself a merchant, and there was some truth in that. He traded in anything nobody else wanted to be associated with; he owned taverns that those who deemed themselves as respectable would never frequent. He disposed of the dead for the parish, furnished three pawn shops with the trappings of the deceased and desperate, provided violence for coin, loaned money and rented poor accommodation to those who could barely afford it. But then someone had to, and Myles was of the opinion that as it had ended up becoming his business, he may as well do as good a job of it as he could. And he did. His various businesses presented him with a good profit.

Devereux recognised progression. A farthing on its own was worthless, but add three more, and you had a penny; two pennies gave you half a groat; add two more, and you had a groat, then collect twelve pennies, and then you can trade them for a silver shilling. Five shillings to the crown, ten to an Angel and twenty to a full pound. And like all good magpies, Myles Devereux was attracted to the shinier of the realm's coinage.

It was the end of the day and he was waiting for a delivery, he toyed with the coins before him, stacking and restacking them and enjoying the solid chink. He was about to trade twenty-five silver shillings for gloves.

Matthew's rapid tap on his door was followed a moment later by the appearance of his capable lieutenant, his face wearing a scowl of disapproval as he announced, "Drew's here."

Myles suppressed a smile. "Well then, send him in."

Drew brought the package himself, attended by one of his apprentices who hovered behind the tailor.

Myles ran his eyes over the tailor. He'd put on weight, and he was better dressed than usual. Trade was obviously profitable. Myles cast a quick glance at the stack of coins, a pained expression on his face. Was he paying Drew too much?

"I received them back last night, Master Devereux, and I am hoping you will be pleased with them." Drew stepped towards Myles' desk and reverently placed the silk parcel before him. Myles admired the extravagant wrapping for a moment: burnished golden-brown cloth neatly folded and tied with a double thread of shining thick black thread. Myles licked his lips involuntarily, Drew didn't miss his look of pleasure and smiled.

The top of the soft parcel was tied with a neat and enticing bow, the ends of the cords tempting him to pull them. Myles took one in each hand and tugged gently. The bow slithered silently away undoing the knot below, the silk released, yielded, opening to reveal the gloves.

Drew had chosen his fabrics well. The gloves were a combination of velvet and soft leather, black upon black, the perfect setting for the gold and pearl design that adorned the back of each.

“Please, Master Devereux, try them,” Drew said, his voice a whisper.

Myles didn’t look up, enjoying the vista before him far too much. He lifted the right glove and pressed his hand into it. A further sensory delight was delivered by the unseen soft lining that slid over his skin, seemingly moulding the glove to his hand. The fit was perfect, and the length was as he had directed.

Myles smiled.

The gloves were exquisite. Soft supple leather dyed black with fine stitching picked out with gold thread. Myles slid his hand into the left one and held the pair out before him. The embroidery emphasised the length of his fingers, and the long gloves fitted neatly over his narrow wrists, a gold button fastening on the underside drawing the cuff to a snug fit. On the backs of the gloves, his initials were finely embroidered in more gold thread, and the letters were highlighted with iridescent pearls. They were costly, extravagant and perfect. When Drew had recommended the glover he had been uncertain.

“And here is the second pair,” Drew said, confidence in his voice now he had seen Myles’ pleasure with the first pair he had presented.

The second pair were also beautifully wrapped, and if the first pair had been a delight the second pair were pure joy. The contrasts were striking. Black leather, crusted with a red fire created from the rubies prised from a church hoard he had acquired. The stones had been arranged to form a heraldic image which bore a striking resemblance to that of the Earl of Devon, Edward Courtney. Myles Devereux, shared lineage with the Earl through a cousin. The connection was known, and Myles actively promoted the rumour. However, this was the first time he had adopted a heraldic device. It was more than indiscreet; it was blatantly flouting the Sumptuary laws. Some minor variations in design to distinguish it from the Earl’s device had been sufficient to satisfy the glover’s conscience, but it was still a blatant duplication.

Matthew had expressed his concerns, but Myles, filled with confidence over the recent defeat of a rival, Tasker, wasn’t interested in listening. Tasker’s wealth, which now fell under Devereux’s control, was a huge hoard of Catholic church trappings that had been diverted from old King Henry’s coffers during the rape of the monasteries. Whether they had been hidden to save them or stolen would never be known. However, disposing of them and turning them into tradeable commodities remained problematic.

In their present form, their origin was plainly obvious, and trading in Church wealth, worse, stolen Catholic gold, would receive a blunt and terminal sentence from the current monarch. He couldn't smelt it; there was too much, and the market for stolen gold, which he was well acquainted with, would take only a tiny amount of what he had. Trying to trade more would only raise suspicions.

So, Devereux, stuck on how to dispose of it, was at the moment trading in what parts of it he could. Many of the items were decorated with gems, both real and glass, plus a large quantity of pearls. He had removed and sorted these, and over the coming year, he could supply them in small amounts to tailors, buttoners, and jewellers. Six, ten, twelve, or twenty matched stones could be used to ornament buttons and gowns.

He'd argued with Matthew that he might as well use the rubies himself on the gloves rather than keeping them in a coffer; there were, after all, more than he could sell. Matthew couldn't argue with that, although he still didn't like Myles' use of the stones.

Matthew knocked on the door again, ruining Myles' enjoyment, and he bestowed a hard glare on the man. "What?"

"Uttridge is here," was all Matthew said, resting a disapproving gaze on the gloves.

Uttridge was Myles Devereux's lawyer. "I didn't think anything would prise that limpet from his offices at this time of day."

Matthew shrugged and cast a disparaging glance over Drew and his assistant. "Well, it has, and he's here."

Myles let out a long, noisy breath, his eyes switching between the gloves and the coins. "Here, Drew, take this. I've business to attend to."

Myles prodded the neat stack of shillings with a long-gloved forefinger, sending the pile to slew across the desk. A nimble and quick man, the tailor darted forward and swept the coins from the table before any were lost to the floor. Bowing quickly and gesturing to his attendant, Drew retreated.

"Shall I send him in?" Matthew queried, holding the door open to allow the tailor to scurry from the room.

"Make him wait," Myles said, already returning his eyes to the gloves on the desk. Matthew, shaking his head slightly, closed the door.

One of Devereux's taverns had burnt to the ground, and he wanted to rebuild it on a larger scale. Uttridge was dealing with the necessary land acquisitions. No doubt the man had some query he felt inadequate to deal with on his own. Myles spent some time replacing the gloves inside their silk parcels and resecuring the threads that held them inside their soft cocoon before he sent for Uttridge.

Once Uttridge had been part of a legal firm at Lincoln's Inn, but when his gambling debtors had arrived at his employer's door seeking payment, he had found himself quickly turned off. He had sought a loan from Devereux to prevent him from having his bones broken, and since then, he had worked for him. He was useful, and even Matthew had to admit, it was cheaper to keep Uttridge on than seek the services of a legal firm when he needed it. Uttridge also leant a degree of weight to his dealings with the parish, producing contracts that gave Myles' business an air of respectability. He also drafted loan agreements and dealt with anything else Devereux handed him.

His lawyer arrived with his usual sense of self-importance and the habitual sheaf of papers beneath his arm that Myles had yet to see him refer to. He was trailed by a nervous youth carrying a portable table and a scribe's bag.

Myles folded his arms and looked towards the lanky lad weighted down with the trappings of Uttridge's trade. "Are you really intending to set up a temporary office before me, or are we about to hold court?"

Uttridge swivelled towards the boy and said defensively. "I thought we may need a scribe."

"We very well may need one. I don't yet know, Uttridge, what is on your mind. However, I do know that you can write, and so we can dispense with the scribe," Myles addressed the boy. "Leave your wares here, should your master need pen and ink, and scurry off to the taproom."

The boy hid a smirk at Devereux's comment beneath his hand. Collecting his wits, he straightened his face and slid the straps from his shoulders. The portable table landed with a dull thud on the carpet. Myles rolled his eyes.

"Yes, yes, go on, James," Uttridge said, shooing the boy towards the door. He took hold of the portable table, an ungainly contraption that used heavy hinges to unfold and form a small table and a seat for the writer. He attempted to move it to the side of the room; the wooden sides began to part now that the leather strap had been released, and Myles watched, shaking his head as Uttridge dragged it across the floor, rucking the carpet as he went. Finally he stopped, and pressed the two halves firmly back together, catching his fingers in between the wooded edges and emitting an unintelligible curse of complaint.

"Are you quite finished?" Myles asked.
Uttridge straightened, turned and took a step towards Devereux. His motion was abruptly halted by the fold of his lawyer's robe caught in the brass hinges of the table.

Myles pressed his lips together hard, thought for a fleeting moment about not laughing, and then abandoned the idea. Uttridge, red-faced now, tried to tug the material free, but it was caught fast within the table's mechanism. He was forced to place his pile of documents on the floor so he could use both hands to secure his escape.

"Free yourself, or drag it over here with you ... either will be a pleasure to watch," Myles said, continuing to laugh; he'd hitched himself up onto the end of the desk.

"A moment, sir," Uttridge said, trying to regain his composure and his cloak but failing. Tugging at the top of the wooden box, he managed to get it to fall open, and the metal hinges unclamped their jaws from his gown. He began to try to heft the two halves back together.

"Pray, Uttridge .... leave it. If I do need a scribe, you'll be of little use to me with your fingers missing," Myles said, wiping a tear of mirth from his eyes and then adding, "I shall recommend you to Matthew next time the players attend. Tell me, what has caused you to drag your office to mine?"

Clayton Uttridge, a hole in his legal robes and his self-esteem also a little ragged, stood before his master, his cap clasped in his hands, and smiled nervously at his employer. His papers, reclaimed from the floor, were once again tucked beneath his arm.

Uttridge pulled the sheaf of papers from underneath his arm, opened it and, selecting one, held it towards Myles. "You've been summonsed to appear before William Harpur, Sheriff of London."

"What!" Myles dropped from the edge of the desk, any amusement at Uttridge's plight of a moment ago, gone from his face, he snatched the paper from the lawyer's hand. "Why?"

"There's an allegation of false imprisonment, a writ of habeas corpus has been issued, and you have been summonsed to disprove ...."

"False imprisonment!" Myles blurted, his face wearing an expression of open surprise.

"If you'll please let me finish, sir, it is being alleged that you are holding the person of Lord Fitzwarren and keeping him imprisoned against his will at his home in London, and you are summonsed to present yourself at the sheriff's office," Uttridge delivered the words quickly, the man was clearly nervous, clenching the material of his cloak tightly in one sweaty hand.

"I'm not bloody well presenting myself anywhere – do you hear?" Myles retorted furiously, setting off to circle the room. "What else does it say?"

"Nothing else, it's all very straightforward; you are summonsed to attend with ...."

"Summonsed to attend! Who's made this allegation!" Myles demanded, his eyes still on the paper in his hand, scanning the neat lines of Latin legalese for clues.

"I don't know, sir," Uttridge replied, taking a hasty step backwards.

"Tell me what you do know then?" Myles demanded.

"Well, the writ has been signed and filed by Geoffrey Clement; he's a lawyer who keeps his own office away from Lincoln's Inn," Uttridge replied nervously. "The allegation is made in the name of Lord Fitzwarren."

"I can't believe that!" Myles countered, waving the writ towards Uttridge. "The old man may not like me, but he knows he would be a fool to dispense with my protection. This is of someone else's making. Who's this Clement?"

"I've not had too many dealings with him before. He tends to work on his own and ..."

"Come on, Uttridge, what is it you don't want to tell me?" Myles demanded.

"I don't know if he still is, perhaps not, but he used to work for ..."

"For God's sake, man," Myles snarled, stepping towards the lawyer.

"He is .... or maybe was .... I don't know if he still works for him, but ...."

"Get on with it!" Myles growled in Uttridge's ear. "The name?"

"Bennett .... Garrison Bennett ...." Uttridge stammered.

Garrison bloody Bennett!

"How long has this lawyer been working for Bennett that you know about?" Myles demanded

"Quite a few years, I suppose, I came across him when the landlord of the Black Ship Tavern, Stephen Turner died, do you remember?" Uttridge replied.

"Oh, I remember quite well! That piece of shit, Bennett, produced a bloody heir to inherit, and the place is now controlled by him when it should have been mine in payment for that dead bastard's debts!" Myles spoke through clenched teeth, his eyes as dark as jet.

"Yes, quite, and that was three years ...."

"No, it was two years ago, and his lawyer outwitted you, if I remember rightly," Myles stated coldly.

"There was little I could do, Master Devereux. They had an heir, a final testament, there was nothing we could do to refute it," Uttridge said hastily, his voice rising a pitch.

"You should have anticipated it. That's what I pay you for. Turner should have signed the Black Ship over before he died; then, Bennett could have done nothing—an unsecured debt is a bloody worthless debt, remember that," Myles spoke the words with a cold derision.

Uttridge, observing his feet, did not reply. Myles just stared at Uttridge, who paled even further. "You have a task, Uttridge. Find out who is behind this. If it is Bennett, I want to know."

Uttridge nodded rapidly, the movement rattling the papers beneath his arm.

"Well, don't just stand there. Get to it," Myles snapped when Uttridge didn't move.

Uttridge swallowed hard. "Master Devereux, there is another matter that I do require your signature for."

Myles looked to the ceiling and cursed under his breath. "What now?"

Uttridge shuffled through his clutch of papers. "Eldrich Slouch, sir, he owes you six shillings."

"And?" Myles cut in.

"Well, sir, I need to place a claim against his estate so that when his financial affairs are settled …."

"Slouch is dead?"

Uttridge nodded. "Indeed, some days ago, sir. I thought you might have heard. He has no family or heir, and what he does have, he has gifted to the church. I just need your signature here," Uttridge found the relevant sheet and placed it on the desk, stepping quickly back away.

Myles pulled the paper roughly towards him, found a pen, dipped it, and added his signature at the bottom of the page with his usual flourish before discarding the sheet. Uttridge produced a small pot of pounce from inside his robe, stepped forward, tipped some onto the sheet, swirled it around and discarded it to the floor.

Myles glared at the grit falling onto his carpet before returning his gaze to Uttridge, who paled. "Are you quite finished?"

"I need to reply to the sheriff. An appointment has been made, and a response is required," Uttridge said weakly.

Myles turned, walked towards his open window, and stared into the yard. "What are my choices, lawyer?"

"Well, sir, you need to attend. If you don't, then the sheriff can issue a warrant for you to be presented to him, and that would be …." Uttridge let the words trail off, not wanting to mention the recent events when Devereux had been arrested.

"What if I attend and bring the old shit with me? Will that suffice?" Myles replied.

"Indeed, sir, that would resolve the issue immediately; if Lord Fitzwarren gives a testimony that he is not held against his will in person, then the matter would rest," Uttridge replied.

"Good. Then I shall attend …. And you, master lawyer, can come with me," Myles said turning back to face Uttridge. "Now, get out and take that contraption with you."

Uttridge, pleased to be dismissed, scuttled across the room and began to heft the wooden table from the floor. He slung the strap around his neck, losing his hold on the papers beneath his arm. A flurry of parchment dropped at Uttridge's feet.

"Out! Now!" Myles marched to the door, hauling it open. "Matthew!"

Matthew stepped inside, his gaze following Myles' outstretched arm towards the clerk's table. Matthew lifted it easily, exchanged a brief word with the retreating Uttridge, and dropped it on the floor in the outer room before retracing his steps.

"I assume you heard what Uttridge said?" Myles demanded as soon as Matthew closed the door. "What do you think?"

"I think we should find out if Clement is still Garrison's lawyer," Matthew replied thoughtfully.

"I agree. That cur would like nothing more than to see me publicly humiliated! But how did he find out about Fitzwarren?" Myles said, his arms thrown wide.

Matthew shook his head. "I don't know, but I don't suppose it would be that hard. Depends on who he has watching us at the moment. If he's seen your men posted at the old Lord's house and they've spoken to a few servants, it wouldn't be difficult to find out what's going on."

Myles looked thoughtful. "Or he's had some contact with Robert Fitzwarren, that's a man with an axe to grind. Either way, I'll not dance for the delight of Garrison Bennett."

Myles tapped his fingers along the chair back for a few moments before he spoke. "Get a few more men at Fitzwarren's house and find out about this lawyer, Clement."

"Do you want me to call on him?" Matthew ventured.

"Not yet, let's find out what's going on first," Myles replied continuing to pace the room. "None of the news today is good. Did you know Slouch was dead?"

"The botcher?" Matthew asked.

"The same. Another dead debtor left his money to the church; that'll be six bloody shillings I'll not see again," Myles grumbled.

"You'll have greater problems than losing six shillings if you don't present Fitzwarren. It would be a good idea to make sure the old shit is going to sing the right song?" Matthew said bluntly, then pointing a finger towards Myles he added, "First task for the morrow."

Myles scowled at his back as he left the room, knowing he was right. Then he felt another pair of eyes upon him. Turning, he found Amica staring at him from the sill. Myles smiled at the perfection of the image. The window framed the cat, and behind her was the tower of St Bride's. Behind that, split perfectly by the spire, was the full moon, illuminating the Church and bringing into sharp relief the outline of Amica. Myles settled back in his chair and wondered if she'd jump from the sill to his desk and then stalk across the floor arrogantly before climbing onto his lap, or would she disappear into the night, prowl the deserted streets and return later with a dead mouse to deposit on his pillow. His plate was still close; carefully cut pieces of cheese sat on the edge, waiting for the cat.

Myles picked one up and held it out. "Do you want this?"

The cat switched its gaze to his hand and the offering but made no move to enter the room. Myles was about to discard the cheese back onto the plate when Amica, her decision made, moved with the speed of a falcon from sill to desk to floor and jumped silently into his lap. Her tail flicked across his face, the fur tickling his cheek. Smiling, Myles opened his hand, and Amica took the cheese. He ran his hands along her back, and purring, she pressed against his touch, turning until she was curled up happily in his lap.

Myles let out a long breath and addressed the cat. "Today is not turning out to be a good one."

Uttridge's news had tarnished what should have been a pleasurable end to the day, the silken packets of gloves were now forgotten on the desk.

Chapter 2

"It seems we have a problem," Myles said, directing his words to the painting of the woman on the wall and not towards the seated man. He cast lascivious eyes over the image of the man's dead wife, knowing full well how much it annoyed the old Lord.

"What problem?" William Fitzwarren roared, his anger already rising.

"It seems my charity has been cast back in my face," Myles replied tersely.

"Charity!" William scoffed.

Myles turned to regard William with a stern, dark gaze. "Yes, charity. You are here now and not mouldering in the filth at Netley because of my charity."

"I paid you for that, and you damn well know it," William growled.

A look of annoyance crossed Myles' face. "It's not always about profit, although that's always nice. Richard's story of what had happened to you, imprisoned by your son, Robert, while he helped himself to your wealth, genuinely tugged at my heart. A sad tale indeed."

"I find that hard to believe!" William grunted in reply.

"Oh, come now, do you really think me such an uncaring creature?"

William didn't answer.

"Anyway, we do have a problem. Have you heard of Garrison Bennett?" Myles asked, turning his attention from the painting and towards William.

William shook his head.

"It is being alleged that I am keeping you here against your will, a prisoner in your own home, and a writ of habeas corpus has been issued," Myles said, sliding up to sit on the edge of the table.

"Robert! Damn him! I knew this would happen," William said, "I was wondering when he would reappear."

"It may be his doing, it may not be. Either way, I need to produce you at the sheriff's, where you will confirm you are not being held against your will. I cannot see how that would be of any benefit to Robert? He'll know you will hardly deny it, and I doubt you have any plans to cast yourself back into his keeping," Myles finished.

"I don't know, but he's a devious cur. He tried to take control of my property before by alleging I was infirm of mind," William replied, glowering at Myles, who sat perched on the table's edge.

"Well, to be fair, he probably has a point, old man," Myles replied, a malicious grin on his face.

Ignoring his comment, William continued. "I need to talk to my lawyer, Luttrell. He can advise me."

"You'll need to be quick, old man. I need to produce your bag of bones at the sheriff's office tomorrow, whole, hearty and hale – so don't bloody die to spite me!" Myles warned and slid neatly from the polished wood, his boots landing soundlessly on the rugged floor. "We shall arrive together, in companionable accord. I'm sure you'll enjoy the distraction."

Myles rode back slowly, his escort in tight formation behind him. His mare, well-schooled, picked her way back towards the White Hart. Myles had little mind on his journey. The clamorous noise of a water carrier's pewter cups revived his attention, and he realised he was on Clough Street. His annoyance increased. Further along was Slouch's botchers shop, which reminded him about the lost six shillings.

Damn the man.

Elridge Slouch's business had come to him through his wife, who had gone to the grave not long after Old Hal had breathed his last. His botchers shop was the largest in London, and Myles dealt with him occasionally. Eldridge's workshops repaired rips and tears in clothes, but their speciality was to make clothing from the city's rags. Myles disposed of the parish dead, and Eldrige didn't ask any questions when handed a pile of soiled shroud cloths. Myles had considered washing and reselling them, but Matthew had baulked at the suggestion. He was already unhappy that Myles' men unwrapped the dead when they had an opportunity to do so and stripped them of any other clothing they found, but reselling the shrouds of the parish's dead was too much even for Matthew. Myles had relented, only because it might be bad for business. So instead, they were bundled together in an empty stable at the back of the White Hart; when there were enough to fill a cart, they were taken to Slouch, who bought them on weight. Myles was fairly sure Eldridge cleaned and sold them on rather than using them in his botching business, and he tried not to resent the profit Eldridge made that he could have added to his own coffers, but the fact still rankled him.

Any unsold clothing or anything abandoned in Devereux's taverns ended up in Eldridge's. Matthew's rat boys, who worked for their right to live beneath the tavern's roof and feed from the kitchen scraps, would present any cloth they found, which was added to that sent to Slouch. Any man who got drunk and left his cloak wouldn't see it waiting for him on his return.

Myles drew level with the botchers shop. The door to the workshop stood open, and it seemed that business was progressing as usual despite the owner's death. Maybe he was looking at this the wrong way.

The death of Eldridge Slouch provided an interesting opportunity. His wife was dead, he had no children, and what he owned he had left to the church for his divine salvation. And specifically, to St Bride's, where Myles Devereux had an arrangement with the priest, Kemp. During the previous year, when the sweating sickness had been at its height, Devereux, charged with disposing of the bodies, had run short of space and had stored them in the crypt at St Bride's, forcing coins into the hands of Kemp to ignore the practice. In fact, forced was far too strong a word; the hand had been open and eager, and the face it belonged to had been saddened when Myles stopped using the crypt and handing over silver to the priest.

Myles was confident Kemp would be more interested in a fiscal sum from Eldridge rather than the lengthy task of trying to find a buyer. He would make an offer Kemp would be unlikely to decline, especially after he was made aware that he could keep half of the coins for himself. Then Myles would own the botchers workshop and the house attached to it to do with as he wished. It was neat. An outlet for his funerary rags, it was also a business that provided clothes to many of Devereux's clients, and the fact that they were spending money with anyone other than himself was just not acceptable.

It would be profitable.

Myles pulled on the reins, slowing his mare, and brought her to a stop outside Eldrige's shop.

Matthew pulled his mount next to Myles. "What are we stopping here for? Slouch is dead, remember?"

Myles grinned. "That is exactly why we are stopping."

Slouch had lived in a two-story house. To the left at ground level were his workshops, and the yard at the back was roofed to provide more working space. What had once been stables were now crammed with the rags of his trade. Along the end of the property ran Skinners Brook. The banks had been cut away, and two long channels banked with stone slabs were fed by it and used for washing the cloth scraps.

Myles, followed by Matthew, made his way through the botchers shop towards the yard at the back. Two women were pouring ash into the channel from leather buckets, grey dust rising around them like morning mist. The one on the right dumped her bucket and wiped her sleeve across her watering eyes. Her companion had swapped her bucket for a wooden paddle and began to pound the rags and ash mixture.

Devereux recognised the one with the paddle; it was Peggy Delwyn. She'd run the workshops for Slouch; her beady eyes kept the women from idling, and it seemed that it was business as usual in Slouch's absence. Peggy was never still, not afraid of hard work; she always had a basket on her hip or was bent over the sewing tables or, as now, pounding the rags in the channel. Peggy was a short, plump woman who reeked of practicality. Her hair was coiled and tied away beneath a tight-fitting cap, short sleeves meant only her forearms got wet, and around the front of her skirts, an apron made of tightly sewn scraps protecting them from the slurry in the channel. Probably only a handful of years older than Myles, but a lifetime of working with lye had given her skin the look of old leather and her cheeks an unnatural purple tinge.

It was good to know that work was continuing. Myles didn't want to buy empty workshops without workers and nothing to produce. He wanted to buy a living business, and it seemed this was still the case.

A breeze drew away the plume of ash. Myles waited until it had gone entirely before advancing towards the women—his black velvet doublet didn't need a coating of grey. Seeing him, both women stopped and performed clumsy curtsies with the paddles still clutched in their hands.

Myles leant over the channel. The ash had turned the water black, and there was little to be seen of the soaked cloth beneath its surface. "That ash removes the filth from clothes is a contradiction."

The women exchanged glances but remained silent. Myles tried again. "You use the filth from the hearth to clean the filth from the rags."

Confusion continued.

Myles rolled his eyes. "It seems unlikely that fire ash will clean the dirt away."

The look of confusion melted, and Peggy Delwyn said, "Aye, Master Devereux, it does, an' it'll take the skin from your palms as well if you leave them in there too long." She held forward the hand that was not holding the wooden paddle. The palm was as red as freshly sliced. "You'd be better keeping yours inside those fine gloves, sir." Peggy delivered the final words with a wink, earning her a scowl from Matthew.

"I'll heed your advice and keep my hands dry," Myles said, smiling. His eyes strayed for a moment to the rubies on his hands.

"You'd be best to, Master Devereux. Some call it the Devil's flour," Peggy said, pointing towards the bucket of ash. "It's meant to be mixed with holy water, then it'll strip flesh from bones, or so they say, but with water from the brook, it's just strong enough to soak away a bit of grease."

"That, Mistress Delwyn, is an opinion you'd be best keeping to yourself," Myles said.

"Aye I will, but I don't mind tellin' you, Master Devereux," Peggy said laughing.

"And why's that then?" Myles said, his eyebrows raising a degree.

"Black as a star plucked night, ye' are, there's a bit of the Devil in yer, I'm sure," Peggy said, then winked again.

"How dare you, woman!" Matthew stepped towards Mistress Delwyn, his right hand raised, and his intention clear.

"Matthew, stay your hand, Mistress Delwyn, is jesting." Myles said.

Matthew lowered his hand slowly, transferring his displeased look from Peggy to Myles.

Shortly after, Myles was mounted again and headed back towards the White Hart. Myles smiled to himself. What had the woman said. 'Black as a star plucked night.' He liked it. His reservations that Drew's latest offering would not make him stand out from the crowd had been, he admitted, wrong. Running a gloved hand down one of his sleeves, he admired the rich, faultless black of the velvet and silk. He'd not been sure of the design when Drew had suggested it. The slashes in the sleeves revealed a rich black silk below. Drew had extolled the design as emitting a subtle brilliance, but Myles had been dubious. There was little to catch the eye apart from the row of buttons down the front. He would have described the design not as dowdy, but as simple.

Drew, his professional pride dented, had continued to argue his case. The velvet was of the highest quality, combined with the best silk imported from the East, layered three times and gathered with stitches to capture the light. The tailor hadn't even wanted to ornate it with buttons, arguing a bright button would detract the eye from the finery of the garment. Myles had folded his arms and wondered precisely what Master Drew was trying to sell him. Drew's final line had been to point out that Queen Mary's husband, Phillip of Spain, had recently been seen in a similar creation and that the design was of Spanish origin and would, no doubt, be soon very widely copied. That had swayed Myles, and he conceded, with the caveat that he chose the buttons. His eyes strayed to the gloves and the glinting rubies; he'd liked them, but now he wasn't so sure. Maybe Drew could advise on another design.

Despite the summons to the sheriff, Myles was feeling better. Indeed, he'd charge the old shit for tomorrow's excursion; Myles Devereux was not summonsed anywhere. However, he would bill Lord Fitzwarren for his lawyer's fees, which would be sizeable. None of which would be going to Uttridge.

"Did you hear me?"

Matthew's words broke through Myles' reverie, and he bestowed an annoyed gaze on the rider next to him.

"I see you didn't. Why did we stop at Slouch's?" Matthew questioned.

Myles twisted in his saddle, smiled, and waved a hand. "Here's to Good Old King Hal. God rest his rotten soul."

"What are you talking about?" Matthew moved his horse closer to Myles' mare.

"Slouch, of course," Myles said, smiling. "I want his business."

"If you can secure it, his botchers shop would be a worthwhile addition," Matthew said, for once in agreement, then added. "How will you make the deal?"

"Henry paved the way for me on this occasion when he started to strip the land holdings from the church," Myles replied.

Matthew laughed, without humour. "What was it they used to say, a thousand years of husbandry undone in a hundred days by his lackey, Cromwell."

"True, but it's stopped Mortmain," Myles said.

"Mortmain?" Matthew said, his brow furrowed.

"It translates, Matthew, as dead hand. The church could take property into their hands, hands that would never die, could never be disinherited, and worse, for greedy old Henry, couldn't be taxed. You are right; Cromwell sliced through all that swiftly enough," Myles mused, then added, "Land for the church is problematic, and a botchers shop would be even worse, but a small pile of chinking coins will be more convenient," Myles concluded.

"And do you think you'll succeed?" Matthew said.

Myles smiled. "I don't see why not."

"That woman, Delwyn, she's a cheeky wench. You'd be better off without her. She's trouble, I can smell it," Matthew said.

Myles frowned. "She's run Slouch's workshop for years, knows the business, and is a hard worker. What's she done to upset you?"

"She's getting above herself," Matthew said bluntly.

"Ah," was all Myles said in return.

Matthew looked at his employer disapprovingly. "Don't be won over by her words. She might play the fool for you, but she's a conniving woman. How else did she manage to run Eldrige's business? There's nothing to say she's not taking a profit from it herself. You'd be better off without her."

Matthew had taken a dislike to Peggy Delwyn, and Myles knew from experience that his opinion would be unlikely to change. "In time, Matthew, perhaps, but for now, Mistress Delwyn stops where she is. If you are overly concerned after the deal is done, you can send one of the men to oversee the workshop."

Matthew rolled his eyes. "I'll have men falling over themselves when they find out they are guarding a bloody wash-house."

"If you don't want them to suffer, then go yourself," Myles replied, then his attention wandered to a man ahead of them, uncomfortably astride a sizeable horse and making slow progress down the street, his bulky body swaying dangerously with every step his mount took.

Justice Daytrew. The day was getting even better.

Daytrew was the Parish Justice, a position he had to have paid for; there was little chance he could have obtained it on merit. He was a man who wore his self-importance like a peacock's plumage. It had been Myles' misfortune to have crossed his path several times already this year, and on the last occasion the justice had been on the losing side.

Myles pressed his heels into his mare's flanks and closed the gap, pulling his horse up next to the justice's.

Daytrew's grimace when he heard Myles' voice was satisfying, and Myles let a grin slide onto his face. He had little to fear from Daytrew, a few months ago he had caught men Daytrew had set to guard the scene of a murder charging an entry fee for those inclined to view the deceased. Leaning closer to Daytrew and receiving the unwanted scent of Daytrew's sweat, Myles said, "You've new men I see, hopefully better than some you have employed in the past."

Daytrew reddened immediately, the reminder unwanted and jewels of sweat were beginning to arrange themselves along the fat creases on his forehead.

"If you will excuse me, Justice Daytrew, I've much to attend to," Myles said; having made the justice suffer sufficiently, he pressed his horse forward and ahead of Daytrew, his own men jostling quickly past the justice to keep up with their master.

An image of a butchers with heads from the kills, a proclamation as the freshness of the meat, wandered into Myles' head. Each butcher used a different decoration in the animals' mouths; some hung from them dry straw rings, others bunches of fresh green rosemary or thyme and in the colder months, dried bunches of the same, Old Menson on Birch Street forced a giant stained carved apple into the lifeless jaws. The butcher near Denyson's Yard, who possessed a strange sense of humour, dangled the animal's pizzle from the teeth. Daytrew would not look out of place similarly displayed. Myles grinned.

Susie, on her knees, was lighting the fire, and Amica was pressing against her arm as she did. "You'd think I'm lighting this for you the way you carry on."

The cat meowed a reply, and Susie laughed.

"Who else would you be lighting it for?" Myles said absently from where he was seated at the desk.

"That cat of yours has no idea how lucky it is," Susie said, rising and dusting her skirts before moving towards the bed.

Myles watched as she removed the warming pan and slid something beneath his pillow. "I hope that's not treats for the damned cat that you are leaving in my bed."

Susie reddened. "Sorry, Master Devereux. It's just this," she held up a small linen bag, neatly sewn, saying haltingly. "I used to make 'em for my boy when he couldn't sleep." When Myles just stared at her, Susie's eyes dropped to the floor, and she said defensively, "I paid wi' my own coin."

"That's not .... I didn't ....mean," Myles said badly, then gathering his wits said. "Thank you, but why?"

"I know you don't sleep well, an' I just thought it might help?" Susie said, her eyes on the carpet.

"How do you know I don't sleep well? Who told you that?" Myles snapped, his eyes cold.

"No one had to tell me, your bed looks like a battlefield some days. No-one who has a night of God blessed sleep twists their sheets like that," Susie replied.

"Oh ...." Myles said, then, "Thank you. It is a kindness."

Susie slipped the bag rapidly beneath his pillow, lifted the warming pan, bobbed an awkward curtsey, and before he could say anything else she'd gone.

Carefully, his long fingers twisted the buttons on the doublet, freeing them from the fastenings. Reclining on one of the pillows on the bed, Amica watched him with her steady yellow gaze. The strong scent of lavender wrapped around him. The linen usually smelt of woodruff, but this was something much headier. Lifting his head, he raised the pillow and released a waft of the delicate fragrance. Below was a small bag, plain linen tied closed with a brown cord. Myles pressed it to his nose and inhaled deeply; then, smiling, he slid the bag back and put the pillow on top.

Chapter 3

Later that day, Matthew found out what Myles wanted to know.

"Well, then, Matthew, have you found out what that pariah, Bennett, is up to?" Myles asked, his eyes narrowing and preparing himself for bad news.

"He still uses Clement for his legal work, debt collection, and, you are not going to like this, Uttridge was right; he was the lawyer who provided all the documents when Stephen Turner died, that handed the Black Ship Tavern to Bennett. Clement drafted the final testament, and the document was witnessed in his offices. He executed the transfer deeds that ensured it went to Turner's heirs," Matthew said, folding his arms across his broad chest.

Myles' face darkened. "The will, the witnesses?"

"Everything has Clement's stamp on it," Matthew nodded, his mouth pressed into a thin line. "It only confirms what we already knew, that Bennett cheated his way into ownership of the Ship."

"This writ of Habeas Corpus must be Bennett's doing, it has to be, but why?" Myles replied, "What does he hope to achieve?"

"It could be he thinks you are keeping the old man a prisoner in his home, and forcing you to publicly bring him to the sheriff's office will mean you will lose control of him and his property," Matthew reasoned.

"It could be. The old man thinks this is his son's doing, but I can't see what advantage he would gain. William is hardly likely to want to remove himself from my protection and place himself back into his son's hands, is he?"

"Bennett might know what we use Fitzwarren's house for?" Matthew suggested carefully.

Myles' eyes quickly lifted to Matthew's face. "He had better not know about that."

Myles had recently taken possession of a hoard of church wealth. If it were found, Myles did not wish it to be connected to him, so keeping it close at the White Hart was not a good idea. Instead it was housed in a locked tack room at Lord Fitzwarren's London house.

"It's always a possibility, no matter how careful we've been," Matthew replied, hands up palms towards Myles.

"You picked the men involved yourself. Not a word of this was to be breathed by any of them," Myles replied, a warning note in his voice.

"I did, and I trust the lads, but that doesn't mean that Bennett's not had men sniffing around; he might not know exactly what we are doing, but he might suspect we are using the Fitzwarren house for something more than just looking after the old shit," Matthew said defensively, then added. "Remember, I told you it was a folly to keep those church trinkets."

Myles, ignoring Matthew's accusation said, "Tell Uttridge I want to see him. He had better make sure tomorrow goes my way, or he'll be swimming in a bottomless pool of regret. And I want to talk to him about Slouch."

"I will, and I have these for you," Matthew fished inside his doublet and, a moment later, dropped a leather purse on the desk before Myles. "There you go, that's what Davey has pulled off this week."

Myles picked up the purse, hefted it, and met Matthew's eyes. "Not much, then?"

"They've had the easy pickings, but what's left is harder to remove," Matthew said in defence of Davey.

"Hmm," Myles loosened the strings and poured the contents onto the desk before him. His brows rose and he looked aghast at the offerings that had poured from the purse. Several of the gems were cracked in half, and some were severely chipped. Myles stared at them aghast. "God's bones! Have you seen these?"

Matthew looked down at the glittering pile. "Yes, I have, and a couple are damaged, but they could be recut; it's not that bad."

"A couple!" Myles' voice was high pitched and with a long forefinger he began to slide the damaged jewels to the right of where the purse lay. "Shattered, broken .... chipped .... cracked .... chipped .... ruined ..... half-missing .... chipped .... chipped .... scratched ..... broken ...."

By the time he had finished, there were five times as many in the damaged pile. "For the love of all that is holy, Matthew, whoever you have working on removing these, get them to stop. A blind child with a hammer could do a better job."

"Like I said, they are not as easy to remove as you might think," Matthew grumbled in reply.

"Find someone with some skill," Myles said, an appalled look on his face as he viewed the wasted gems.

"I thought you wanted to keep knowledge of these to ourselves? I can't just get a jeweller to remove them, can I? Not without risk of him having a loose tongue," Matthew said, throwing his arms wide. "My lads are skilled at many things but this is difficult work."

"Difficult!" Myles repeated incredulously.

"Aye, Davey Langton slipped yesterday trying to prise your baubles apart and stabbed himself in the eye."

"That was fortunate. It will at least prevent him from any further ruination," Myles said acidly.

"Davey Langton is one of my good men, and having him sit in the yard with a poultice strapped over his eye isn't helpful. He oversees the markets at the Swan. Now I'm going to have to go. I can tell you, it's left me short-handed," Matthew continued to grumble.

Myles gazed at Matthew. "He's got another eye! He can still ride a horse, can't he?"

"I'll not argue with you," Matthew said, and stabbing the broken gems with a thick finger he added, "and you find someone to pull these damned things apart. I'll not have any more of my men wasted."

Myles laughed incredulously. "I'm hardly asking them to risk their lives! If Davey Langton can't be trusted with a bloody awl it's not my fault."

"Aye, well, that might be right. But you'll need to find another way of doing it. It's no job for the lads," Matthew conceded.

Myles tugged his chin thoughtfully. "Let me think on it, and in the meantime, please get them to put down their hammers!"

Matthew, still grumbling, pulled the door closed hard behind him as he left. The weather was foul outside, and he had no desire to cross London to stop the process of butchering the gems, but he would have to.

Myles poured the poor offerings back into the purse, no longer wishing to witness the destruction that had been wrought by carelessness.

It was a job for nimble fingers. He needed not just agile fingers; he needed them to keep their tongues still as well. He knew plenty of thieves, pick-locks and pocket-dippers, all of whom possessed the necessary dexterity; however, none could be trusted. A common failing of the thieving class, unfortunately. Someone would come to mind; he was sure of it.

Myles was awake early the following day, keen for the day's proceedings to begin. Eager to find out what the outcome would be and who was behind the writ. He was sure that Lord Fitzwarren would confirm he was not being held against his will, but whether he would find out how these charges had arisen in the first place remained to be seen.

On arrival at the Fitzwarren house, Myles was pleased to find that William, too, was ready for whatever the day would hold. His servant had dressed him as befitted his station; the chains around his neck seemed overly heavy, and the rings on his fingers a little slack, but the overall impression was perfect. It was Lord Fitzwarren, confidant of the dead king, Lord of the realm, controller of land from the borders to the south coast, and he'd chosen his clothes well. Red velvet, slashed with a deep blue and trimmed with gold threads graced the aged frame, perfectly contrasting to Myles' in saturnine black. On this occasion, Myles was not at all saddened that he was being outshone; after all, the jewel that would be attracting the attention belonged to him.

Myles had provided a litter for his aged companion. The interior was furnished with sumptuous cushions, velvet drapes in rich damask were tied back so everyone could see who it was that Myles Devereux was accompanying through London. The litter belonged to the head of the Loriners Guild, Master Camberwick, who had borrowed money from Devereux, and the loan of the litter was a small price to pay to ensure no one else knew about the transaction. Owing money to someone as notorious as Devereux wasn't ideal for the newly appointed Camberwick.

Myles very much wanted to be seen with William Fitzwarren, so he rode close to the litter and kept up an almost friendly conversation during the journey. William had not seen London for years, and his eyes darted around with the curiosity of a stranger, and Myles supplied the narrative.

"How long has that been there?" William asked, pointing to the new water conduit in Creston Street. Two water carriers were filling their wooden barrels from it as they passed, their eyes resting on the litter for a moment before dropping back to their tasks.

"A few years, old man; there's much you have missed," Myles said, a smile on his lips.
A little further on were the charred timbers and walls of The Unicorn tavern, a mass of

blackened debris that the weeds had yet to inhabit. Myles tried not to scowl at the remains of one of his most profitable taverns. Seeing William's gaze lingering on the debris, he leaned down a little in his saddle.

"The result of a lightning strike a little over a month ago," Myles said, some of the lightness of a moment ago gone from his voice.

William didn't have the chance to reply, the litter jolted to the right as the carriers moved away to give a wide berth to a flat-bed wagon, drawn by a sagging-backed nag with protruding hip bones as it passed them going in the opposite direction. The wagon back was covered with rough hessian sacking from beneath which poked four pasty white feet.

"The sweating sickness is still rife, especially in the streets near the river," Myles said, pressing a linen kerchief across his face. William sat back in the litter, observing the corpses from beneath knitted brows. "I didn't know London had been gripped by the sickness again."

"I am sure much has happened, old man, that no one thought to tell you about," Myles said.

The accuracy of Myles' observation clouded the old man's face, and some of Myles' good humour returned, and he took up his role of guide once more. "When we turn into Bessinghall Street, you'll see the new front they've put on the Guildhall. It's known as London's new eyesore, and rumour has it the queen is not amused by the merchant's dressing their meeting rooms up like a gilded palace." Myles paused for a moment. "I've heard a story that you pulled the guild master from his chambers here and brought him to his knees in the street. Is that true?"

William made a sound that might have been meant to be a laugh but instead sounded like a harsh rattle in the back of his throat. Myles winced at the noise. "I didn't drag him out. Carter was his name, and I didn't soil my hands. I had him dragged out for me."

"What was his crime? Sending bad wine to old Hal?" Myles asked, grinning.

William shook his head. "No, it wasn't the wine he sent that was the issue; it was the reckoning."

"The bill?" Myles asked intrigued.

William nodded. The harsh cough-like noise rattled around the back of his throat again before he spoke. "Carter sent a revised bill for goods to the king. Tried to charge more than he'd agreed with the king's provisioner and made the mistake of boasting that even the king was not above being affected by rising prices."

"And someone obviously told Henry," Myles said, amused.

"Indeed. Bloody mercers," William spat into the street.

"I class myself amongst that poor breed. However, I have as yet to challenge a king. I'm still working my way up through the noble ranks, and have only made it to your level," Myles said acidly,

"Hah! You! A merchant? You trade only in threats and lies," William growled back.

"Words, as I am sure you are aware, can sometimes be most costly," Myles replied, gripping his reins a little tighter, the mare responded, shortening her stride, her neck arching.

William shook his head and smiled at Myles. "Your mount betrays you."

Myles abandoned his reply, remembering he needed the old man's cooperation, and said, "Age has not robbed you of observation, at least. It's a skill you have passed on to your brood.".

William's brow furrowed. "What do you mean by that?"

"The ability to point out the unwanted," Myles said bitterly, remembering several conversations with William's son, Richard, which he would rather forget.

William hesitated for a moment, confusion blighting his pale face. "What did he say?"

Myles smirked. "That's not the question you wanted to ask, is it?"

"I don't know what you mean?" William blustered.

"You want to know which one of your brood I am referring to? I've not exchanged words with your captor, Robert, so you can discount him, and the blond lacks the wit," Myles supplied.

"The viper, then?" William growled.

Myles shook his head. "It does you no credit to refer so to your saviour, you'd be in Netley now if it hadn't been for him."

"He'll have made a profit, no doubt. I would not be surprised if you paid him, after all this has been a most profitable arrangement for you, hasn't it?" William said.

"Believe what you will," Myles said, a note of boredom creeping into his voice. They were nearing the end of their journey, and he added, "I hope, old man, you are still going to play your part well?"

The proceedings were remarkably brief. William, was interviewed separately from Myles, to ensure there was no hint of duress, he informed the sheriff that his security arrangements for his household were no matter for public concern. His lawyer Luttrell, read out the prepared statement, and the proceedings were closed almost immediately. Myles was left outside the sheriff's offices with his men while William had more than one glass of wine. When he emerged from the sheriff's offices, his gait was a little unsteady, and his cheeks were flushed. He was flanked by the sheriff who was fawning over him, and William was enjoying the attention.

Myles rolled his eyes.

William was helped back into his litter, dropping heavily onto the padded upholstery, and Myles came close to him before the contraption was lifted from the floor, leaning in, his hands on the frame of the litter he said. "Well, old man, what did you learn?"

"Bloody Robert, I told you as much already," William said, a smug expression twisting his age-line mouth into a leer.

"Are you sure, old man?"

"Of course I am. The lawyer was appointed by him, and confirmed to the sheriff he was acting on his behalf," William punctuated his sentence with a brutal laugh. "He wasn't happy about it either?"

"Who? Robert or the lawyer?"

"The damned lawyer. Robert wasn't present, and when I refuted his claims, his lawyer was left looking a fool before the sheriff," William replied with satisfaction.

"Indeed," Myles said. The litter rocking when he pushed himself away from it.

Chapter 4

It should have been a good day. Indeed it had been a good day. So, why did he feel like a rat had been gnawing at his nerves? Robert's lawyer, his professionalism called into question, had been dismissed and sent scuttling from the sheriff's offices. William had played his part, not that he had any other choice. And it was not his rival Bennett who was behind the writ. That should have been enough. It should have been a good day.

Amica made her way across his desk, her tail high. Myles put the pen down and ran his hand along her back as she passed. Silently, she jumped from the desk to the top of a shelf; the landing was not as quiet. The box containing the astrologica was acting as a bookend, and began to slide from the shelf.

The box tipped.

"Amica!" Myles flung his arms out and caught the box just before it fell. He couldn't save the books. Their support gone, the books fell; the final one, its pages flapping like an injured bird reeled over and landed open on the floor.

In his haste to save the astrologica he'd knocked over a candleholder, and wax had spilled across the desk. "Amica, you are the Devil's child. Have a care, damn you!"

The cat, aware of his displeasure, was watching him carefully from the end of his bed.

Myles righted the candleholder. He was about to place the astrologica back on the shelf when he stopped and fixed a dark gaze on the cat. "You'll just do that again, won't you?"

Amical meowed in reply.

Shaking his head, Myles rose and lifted the coffer lid, depositing the box in the bottom before going around the desk to the fallen books.

Reaching down, he picked up the open bible. It topped the untidy heap, the pages creased where it had fallen. Myles picked it up carefully and smoothed the vellum flat. A small piece of folded paper on the floor must have been trapped between the pages. Putting the bible down, he picked it up. Myles unfolded it and stared at the words. Each letter, shakily penned, struck at him like a knife blow.

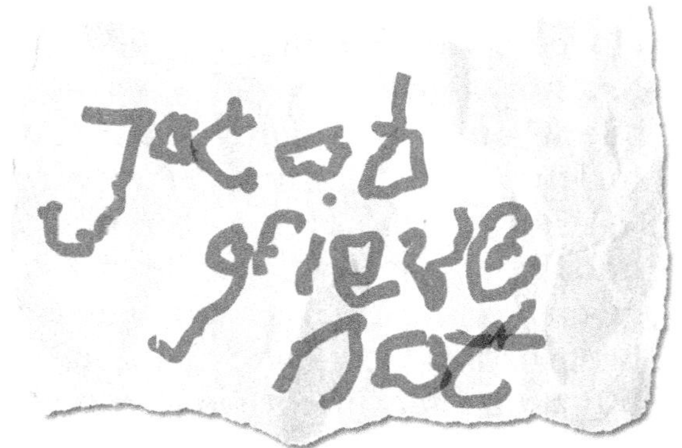

And on the reverse - My peace will be everlasting.

It had been Andrew's bible, his brother's. Picking up the book he opened it again, the front sheet was missing, torn out, and matched the paper that had fallen to the floor. Andrew had been burnt for his convictions. Myles had bribed the guards heavily to send gunpowder to Andrew. The bag of black powder was to have been tied around his neck and would ignite and end his suffering sooner. It was often allowed; the crowd enjoyed the spectacle, and those near the front were often splattered with blood and flesh accompanied by the cheers of the crowd. But not on this occasion. Mary wanted the heretics to suffer, and Myles had been forced to watch the agony of his brother's death. It had been slow, sickeningly so.

Myles felt his knees weaken, and his stomach turned; the feeling was familiar, and he reached out with a shaking hand for the support of the desk. His eyes were tightly closed and yet still filled with the image of his brother tied above the pyre, his scream a silent one; his agony was eternal in Myles' mind. There was never any everlasting peace.

He couldn't look at the note again. Andrew had been the only person to call him by his given name. The last message from his brother, Andrew, who had died two years ago, but it still felt like it was yesterday. The pen in Andrew's hand had shaken as it had penned the words, proof that they had tortured him. Myles had always suspected it but had no way of knowing until now. Those uneven letters, made with hesitant and clumsy lines, told of pain, broken bones and smashed fingers.

Carefully, he replaced the folded message within the pages of the bible and put it back on the shelf, this time away from the edge, so no chance accident could send it to the floor. On the back of a chair was a doublet, the new black one Drew had assured him he would like. Drawing the sleeves on, Myles fastened the buttons slowly.

He'd been writing, and the rings from his right hand were laid on his desk next to the ink pot. He slid them back onto his long fingers and held his hands before him. They trembled still, and his heart seemed to have adopted an irregular beat. His mood was sour when he descended the steps to the tap room of the White Hart.

Myles rarely appeared there. He generally had no desire to sit amongst the tavern patrons. But now, his temper required a release, and there was none in his room. When he was halfway down the steps, the two men on guard at the bottom stood to attention, their eyes on their master. Others in the tap room had noted his appearance, and there was a sudden lull in the level of conversation, enough so that Myles' footfalls on the wooden steps could be heard.

When he was four steps from the bottom, he announced. "I will sit near the fire."

The two men at the bottom knew precisely what this meant, and with brisk efficiency, the drinkers who were sitting near the fire were ousted; the rat boys rearranged the chairs and tables, dragging them away from the fire. Against the wall was a Wainscott chair, oak, heavily carved and used only by Devereux. The top depicted Samael being cast into Hell, and it was known as the Devil's chair amongst those who frequented the tavern. The rat boys hefted the heavy chair across the room, placing it to face the fire.

"Turn it towards the tavern," Myles said quietly. Two of the rat boys jumped to comply, and the chair was lifted and turned, its back now towards the flames. Myles had no desire to rest his gaze upon a fire.

Myles seated himself. Clicking his fingers, he pointed to a small table that was hastily set before him. Myles raised his feet and rested them on the wood, his head resting on the chair's back. He regarded the tavern from beneath his hooded eyes.

One of his men approached, asking. "Master Devereux, can we bring you wine?"

Myles nodded, without looking towards the man.

Wine arrived, silently placed on a small table to his right hand. It had been poured into a garish gold goblet that had been hastily brought from his own room, it had come from Tasker's church hoard.

Myles let his eyes wander over the taproom. It was well filled, which would have pleased him on any normal day. But not today. Matthew, he noted, had arrived; no doubt the men had sent for him, and he was stood near the bottom of the stairs, thick arms folded across his chest, watching Myles. He was the only man in the tavern who had his eyes on Devereux, the rest had more sense and kept their gazes on their meals, their cups or their companions. In time a few would be brave enough to furtively glance in his direction, but not yet.

Myles raised the cup, the metal cold against his lips, and the wine equally chilled, had an edge to it that wasn't pleasant. Maybe the vessel was tainting it? God's bloody Catholic gold was even souring his wine. Myles raised the goblet, tipped it, and watched as the blood red wine poured to spatter on the rushes. When it was empty he released it.

Myles gaze found Rogan, one of the rat boys, where he crouched near the wall. He beckoned the boy forward. “Get rid of that, and bring me a glass.”

Myles, his eyes closed, rested his head back against the chair and listened to the room. The conversation that his arrival had silenced was beginning again, the babble of men’s voices, meaningless words, winding together and creating a gentle noise that filled the void. He could listen to it without having to make sense of it. Like the roll of waves on the beach as they drove their way shoreward, rearranging the shingles, then ebbing and heading back to the sea. A senseless noise, but one that never stopped.

“Master Devereux, it is good to see you this evening.” A voice cut through the wordless babble, it was a painful whine and it pulled at his nerves.

Myles opened his eyes. Before him, was Wybert Grey. Printer, guild member, gambler and frequenter of the Angel.

The foolish printer continued. “I am pleased to have found you, as it happens. I was at the guild yesterday and there is some very lucrative business I would like to discuss. I am sure it will be of interest to you.”

Myles, his eyes on Wybert, never moving his head said. “Is it Friday?”

Confusion crossed Wybert’s face. “Wednesday, sir.”

"So, not a Friday?" Myles said, his voice monotone.

Wybert shook his head.

"Well then. Leave. You do not have my pleasure," Myles said, and closed his eyes. He heard Matthew's quiet orders, and a moment later a grunt of protest as Wybert Grey was briskly escorted from the White Hart.

A clink disturbed him for a second time. It was the noise of a glass being placed on the table next to him. He found it, one of the expensive Venetian ones from his room. The glass was kinder, the edge rounded and smooth, and unlike the golden goblet, the weight was light upon his lips. The wine, though, was the same. Cold, cloying, and with a taste that caught at the back of his throat. Myles swallowed and set the glass down. He knew full well there was nothing wrong with the wine. How could a memory tamper with taste? How could that be?

The tide was turning in the White Hart, and men's voices began to rise, pressing hard on the shingle on the beach. The noise plucked at his nerves, and loud laughter and pointless words, like seals in the water breaching the surface, assaulted his ears.

"I tell yer Sim he were a right bad 'un."

"Next week I said, I'll get it to you then."

"It was this big, I swear."

"I said to 'im, if yer don't pay you don't get."

"Fill that up for me."

Myles lifted the glass of spoiled wine to his lips again, his eyes drifting around the busy room, they stopped when they alighted on a man walking through the doorway of the Hart with two companions.

Dan Wignot.

Tanner.

He was accompanied by two other men, Myles didn't know. He still wore the stained, stinking apron of his trade. His crown of unruly dark brown curls was flattened with a leather cap, the flaps unfastened and swinging against his meaty, unshaven jowls. If the wine had tasted bad before, now it was vile.

Myles glared at the man as he made his way towards an empty bench with his companions. Wignot laughed loudly. Myles winced. The man to his right elbowed him, and Wignot turned and looked towards Devereux. Their eyes met for a fleeting moment, and Wignot looked quickly away, continuing towards the empty bench with his companions. The tanner's face was infused with pink, his unsteady step and overly loud voice lending weight to the fact that the man was already a quart full of ale.

As far as Myles was concerned, Wignot had been told in no uncertain terms, never to grace the White Hart again and his men and removed him from the taproom on Devereux's orders months ago. It seemed, however, that Wignot, in his inebriated state, had decided to ignore the warning and return. Ale bred confidence. Wignot was a big man; his trade gave him strong, muscled arms, and his swagger told of a man who was used to getting his own way.

Myles raised the glass again, thought better of it, and placed it down on the table. The taste in his mouth was sour enough already. He had his mark, now he just needed to wait for the man to make a mistake, and he would, Myles was sure of that.

There was a rustle of the floor rushes, heralding Matthew's approach. Matthew made a pretence of filling the glass. Bending his head close to Myles' ear, he said, "Leave Wignot alone."

"Why?" Myles said, not bothering to look at Matthew.

"There's been enough trouble recently, putting a knife in the tanner's ribs isn't going to help," Matthew warned quietly.

"Who said I was going to use a blade?" Myles replied. "He'll leave here hearty and whole."

Matthew put the wine jug down loudly. "That's alright then."

Having delivered his warning, Matthew straightened and headed back across the room, taking up his post next to two of his other men near the foot of the stairs.

Matthew had been right – Myles did indeed have violence in mind. He ached to break, tear, claw something to pieces. To destroy, as his brother had been destroyed.

Everlasting peace!

Andrew's life had ended in what had felt like everlasting torment. Death had been slow to claim his soul that day. He had died a slow, tormented death, and he may have borne it silently, but he died with the sounds of the shrieks and pitiable wails of those who died tied next to him in his ears.

Wignot had called for ale, his voice loud, the words discordant and rising above the general ebb and flow of the conversation in the taproom. Susie brought it for him promptly enough, and Myles heard his sly words as she placed the cups and jug down before him, and saw the tanners hand lifting her skirts. Wignot, slowed by drink, found his hand closing only on air as Susie neatly stepped past him. Myles' temper had now found another reason to ignite.

One of Wignot's companions produced a worn pack of cards, the faces printed with woodcuts and began to deal them to those seated around the table. Wignot found his purse, fished in it with fat fingers and dropped half a dozen coins on the table. It was a poor game with poor stakes.

A smile found the corner of Myles' mouth and lifted it towards his cheek. With both hands on the chair arms, he rose smoothly and made his way across the tavern towards Wignot and his companions.

Arriving at the table and standing behind the man who sat opposite Wignot, Myles asked, “And the game is?”

The four players exchanged nervous glances, none willing to speak, and the player who had dealt the cards stopped abruptly.

“Well?” Myles prompted, his manner friendly.

“It’s Primero, Master Devereux,” the dealer provided quietly.

Chapter 5

"Primero?" Myles repeated slowly. "I've not played that for a long time. Is there space of an extra player?"

The man who had been seated opposite Wignot immediately removed himself from the bench, sliding to the end and then disappearing into the crowd of customers in the taproom.

"It seems there is," Myles said, smiling. Stepping over the bench, he seated himself at the table. He raised his hand and clicked his fingers, and within moments, his wine glass was placed near his right hand, and an elegant leather purse fastened with a gold cord was set next to it.

"Remind me of the rules, it's been some time since I played Primero. If I remember correctly, there are no eights in the pack," Myles said as he began to release the strings on the purse.

"No eights, nines or tens Master Devereux," the dealer provided. He had reunited the deck and was shuffling the cards.

"Yes, of course," Myles said, smiling. The Court cards score ten points, but I can't remember the rest. Do two to three count as ten plus their value? So a two is twelve points?"

"That's right Master Devereux, a two is twelve points, but it's the cards from two to five that have ten added to their value," the dealer continued to rifle the cards, "and of course the ace is sixteen."

"And sixes and sevens?" Myles asked.

"Ah, those are three times their value, so a seven will be ..."

"Twenty-one, yes, quite. I may have let slip the rules of the game, but my mathematics is still adequate," Myles said, a note of rebuke in his voice. "Come on then, deal."

The dealer gave each of the players four cards. The aim was simple to have the highest score, but on top of that the scores were trumped by certain hands, two or three of the same suit, then the hand Primero, one of each suit, followed by Maximus where the player held the ace, six and seven of the same suit, followed by four cards of the same suit and finally four of a kind. Each of these combinations added additional points to the card values.

Given the complexity of the scoring, it wasn't a game generally played in the taverns. But it suited Myles well, especially as the game was played with a short deck.

Before the players lifted their cards from the table, each slid a coin into the centre. Myles tipped his purse out and, amongst the mess of coins, found a low-value one and, skewering it with a long forefinger, slid it across the table.

They could each swap one card, the discarded ones being placed face up in the centre in a pile and then added to the bottom of the deck when the next game began. Myles folded, the player to the right of the dealer won the game with two pairs, and he nervously pulled the coins towards him.

The dealer dealt again.

Myles lost. He swapped out a six and gained a useless card in replacement, and Wignot, who won the round, declared. “Bad luck, Master Devereux. You’d ‘ave done better there if you’d kept the six.”

“Indeed,” Myles said, forcing a smile onto his face. “As I said. It’s been a long time, but I am sure it will come back to me soon enough.”

Myles’ luck didn’t change, and the purse of coins was now distributed between the other three players, with Wignot holding a disproportionate quantity of Devereux’s money.

Myles called for more ale. More was brought and drunk by those around the table. Myles’ hand did not stray towards his wine glass.

The dealer distributed the cards again, and a few minutes later, Myles, groaning at his bad luck, cast his into the middle of the table. "It seems I am out of practice, lads."

"That last game was close, Master Devereux. You nearly won that one," the dealer said as he collected the cards.

Myles smiled. "Nearly is a long way from a victory. Send me more cards, and let's see if a game will go my way eventually."

And it did.

Myles won the next game and the one after that. Then, betting heavily on his third hand, his new found winning streak let him down and the coins went from the middle of the table to join Wignot's growing pile. They had a large audience now, and everyone in the White Hart was perched on a chair, a stool, a table, or looking over a man's shoulder at the game. It was rare that Devereux was ever seen in his tavern, and no one could remember when he'd involved himself in a game of cards amongst them.

His manner was jovial, his comments amusing, and he seemed not at all worried about his loss of coins. They sided with him, groaning when he lost and hurrahing loudly when he managed to claw back a few coins from Wignot. The other two players had lost more than they could afford and now sat around the table clutching ale cups rather than cards and enjoying the continuing game between Devereux and Wignot. It looked very much like Wignot was going to leave the White Hart as a wealthy man.

Myles called for food and more ale, and both arrived quickly and were distributed without payment amongst those playing and watching the game. If Wignot had entertained any thought of quitting, gathering his winnings, and leaving, it was now doubtful they would let him; he was providing far too good an entertainment.

"More ale! Primero is thirsty work," Myles called again, and then gesturing to the audience packed around him, he added, "and fill their cups as well."

Susie, carrying two jugs, moved among them, pouring ale into eagerly offered cups. Myles raised his eyes from the cards in his hand for a moment and smiled at the scene. Men, grinning, hastily emptied their cups and proffered the dripping empty ones towards Susie for more.

"It's all gone, lads," Susie said tipped the dregs from the jug in her right hand into Sammy Sinter's cup.

"Awww, lass, is that all I'm gettin'," Sammy said, looking at the bottom of his barely wet cup in complaint.

"Woman, go and fetch more," Myles announced, and the men around him let out a loud cheer of approval. Susie met Myles' gaze for a moment; she wasn't smiling, and he was sure there was a spark of anger in her eyes. Myles returned his gaze to the cards, ordered his mind, and shut out the noise around him.

He needed to concentrate if he was going to get this right.

Eight more games were played. Wignot, a fortune before him, and full of ale, made a few slurred comments about ending the game, but his audience wouldn't allow it. Not while there was free ale and entertainment to be had. Hands thumped his back in encouragement, and his wins were hailed with cheers, and Devereux's losses were greeted with sympathetic groans. Myles, who had still not touched his wine, bided his time.

He won the next game by a shallow margin, twenty points to his twenty-three. There had been a victory whoop from around him as the dealer slid a few coins at last back in his direction. The tide was about to change.

Myles' head hurt. His concentration was fixed upon the cards, and it wasn't easy to maintain a pleasant and cordial smile, but so far, he was managing. Two more victories, again small, were greeted with cheers from the surrounding crowd. Then, a loss, a heavy one, and the audience groaned, and words of consolation passed above his head.

The moment was not far off now.

The dealer took the cards in, added them to the bottom of the pack, and sent out four more cards to Wignot and Devereux. For the first time during the night, a moment of nerves assailed Myles as his hand hovered over the cards. Was he right? Had he miscounted? If he had Wignot would be leaving the White Hart a very rich man.

He lifted the cards and let a look of disappointment flit across his face. Wignot might have been drunk, but he had a lot to lose, and he didn't miss it. The tanner drew his cards towards him and keeping them close lifted them and failed to keep a grin from his face.

"Ah, lads, it looks like he's going to take my money again! He has the luck of the Devil himself this night," Myles announced jovially. He took another peek at his cards, grimaced slightly, and said, "Maybe it's time to try and win back a little of my money."

Myles raised his right hand, clicked his fingers, and Matthew set another purse before him. Putting his cards down, he untied the strings and peered into the leather bag. If Wignot thought he was about to reach in and select a coin, he was wrong. Instead, Myles upended the purse, the coins released, slid to the wooden table, and he dropped the purse on top of them before pushing the lot to the centre of the table.

Wignot stared at the glittering pile, his mouth slightly open.

"It's late, Master Tanner, and I'll have one more game to win back my money; if not, you'll leave a wealthy man," Myles said, taking another peek at his cards and grimacing again.

Wignot didn't move. It would take every coin he had taken from Devereux to match what was before him in the middle of the table.

"Come on, man! Ye canna' refuse," one of Wignot's companions, standing at his shoulder, announced, pounding his shoulder to underline his point.

There was a murmur of agreement from the rest of the men crowded behind him. Wignot, placing his cards face down on the table, pushed all the coins he had before him to join the rest that sat between them.

"There ye go, Master Devereux, an' I wish you luck," Wignott said, resting back and retrieving his cards.

Both players could now choose another card. Wignot's hand was good, and Myles was counting on him not risking exchanging a card.

"Are ye' holding, Danny?" The dealer asked the tanner, the pack ready, his hand hovering, ready to dispense the top card.

Danny Wignot smiled. "Not this time, I'll bide with what I 'ave."

"I've not the confidence in my hand that you have, master Tanner," Myles discarded one of his cards and the dealer quickly set the replacement card before him. Myles slid it towards him with a long forefinger, placed his palm over the top and raised the card from the table, and he managed to supress his delight when he stared at the card, bestowing instead a scowl upon the King of Hearts.

"A better hand, perhaps," Myles drummed the fingers of his right hand on the table as he contemplated the cards. "What to do?"

Wignot made a move to lay his cards down, his expression eager. The dealer stopped him. "Master Devereux has not yet made his choice."

"But all the coin is on the table?" Wignot said in consternation.

Myles smiled, He lay his cards face down on the table, and with the fingers of his right hand, pulled a ring from his left and discarded it on top of the pile of coins. "Match me, Master Tanner, or lose all."

Danny Wignot's ale sodden face crumbled. "I've nothing left, sir, you know I canna' match you."

"Oh, but you can," Myles said smiling.

"Wi' what. I've not a coin left in my purse, it's all before you. An' I've no fancy rings to match wi' yours," Wignot complained.

"If you think your hand is good, then your tannery is worth as much as that ring. Pledge that," Myles said, "and if your cards are good you'll not have a need to work again for the rest of this year or next, will he lads?"

There was a chorus of agreement.

"Come on Danny …."

"You've the luck of cards tonight."

"It's a chance you canna refuse."

"Match im' Danny."

Myles let the men around the tanner continue. It was not their livelihoods that were at stake, and their desire to see the end of the game was fuelled by greed and ale. If Danny Wignot won, he'd have a lot more friends tomorrow.

Danny Wignot nodded. "I'll match you."

Those around him pummelled his back and congratulated him as if he'd already won the game.

"Go on, Danny, show 'im what you've got," the dealer said above the noise.

Devereux held up a hand to stop Danny from laying his cards on the table. "No need."

Danny stopped and looked at him in confusion.

"You've two pairs. It's a good hand, especially when two of them are courtly queens," Myles said simply. The smile he bestowed now on the tanner held nothing of good humour. "And the other pair would be worth a total of twenty-six points, a pair of threes."

Danny stared at Devereux. His mouth open.

"But it's not what you have that's important, is it? It's what I hold," Myles raised his wine glass to his lips for the first time since he had joined the card game and emptied the glass.

Silence settled on the tavern as Danny's loose fingers gave up their hold on his cards and revealed a pair of threes and two queens.

Every pair of eyes was now on Myles Devereux, his cards lay face down before him.

Placing the glass down carefully, Myles glared at Danny Wignot. "Make no mistake, master tanner, you played with the Devil tonight, and lost."

Myles flipped over his cards—four Kings. It had taken hours and some sleight of hand to rearrange the deck, but eventually, the puzzle, for that was all it was, had been solved to his satisfaction.

Myles rose suddenly. "Get them out of here, all of them. Now."

Myles's men moved in instantly. They laid claim to the winnings on the table and began to eject the drinkers.

"What about Wignot?" Matthew said to Myles as he walked towards the stairs.

"Keep him here until the morning. We don't want him making off with my winnings, do we?" Myles said smiling.

As he went up the stairs back to his room, Myles met Susie at the top, leaving his room, an empty basket on her hip.

"You've lit the fire?" Myles asked, smiling.

Susie stared at him, her eyes cold, and her mouth set into a thin line. Then, pulling the basket closer and straightening her back, she said defiantly, "Not that you deserve it. A night in the cold might remind you what it feels like."

Shock lifted Myles' brows, and before he could stop himself he found himself asking, "What have I done?"

"Stripped a man of his life, that's what ye did. Put 'im in the gutter for nowt more than yer own amusement," Susie hoisted the basket higher, her chin jutting forwards, and she set off down the stairs before he could say another word.

Myles watched her go, fury on his face. The ungrateful woman only had a roof over her head due to his kindness. He'd deal with her later, now he was aware that the headache was beginning to return, pulling the door open roughly Myles stomped to his room. There he found a poor fire with little life in the hearth, and the fire basket was filled with damp wood, the moss on the bark still wet.

Bloody woman!

Amica, sat on the window sill, her rough tongue smoothing the fur on one of her paws while regarding him with steady judgemental eyes. It seemed even his cat was chastising him!

"And you can stop that as well, just remember who let you in here in the first place!" Myles grumbled towards the cat.

Turning back the covers, Myles was pleased to find that she had at least warmed his bed. It might be June, but the month so far had proved a cold one. A draught of warm air, along with the scent of lavender, drifted up from beneath the sheets. Amica, drawn by the smell and warmth, appeared on the pillow next to him, intent on burrowing beneath the covers.

"No, out .... go on. I'll not have my bed filled with cat fur. Go on, move," Myles waved his hand in annoyance at the cat.

Amica meowed loudly in annoyance and returned to the pillow.

"Good, and stay there," Myles said; closing his eyes, he breathed in the tranquil scent, settled his head into the pillows and stretched his long legs towards the bottom of the warm bed.

Myles let out a screech followed by a string of curses. Flinging the covers back violently, he rolled from the bed. Amica, yowling in fright, darted from the bed. In a single leap, the terrified feline made it from the bed to Myle's desk. She landed hard and slid on top of several loose sheets of paper, which collected an ink pot and sent it to collide with a candle holder, both of which fell and banged on the floor. Emitting another shriek, the cat made it to the windowsill.

"God's bones," Myles hopped on the floor. "I swear I'll kill her."

The pain subsided a little, and Myles descended into one of the chairs near the fire, raising the burnt foot to his knee to examine the damage. At the same moment, Matthew burst through the door.

"It's alright, Matthew; this time, my pain was self-inflicted," Myles growled, looking at the long red line on the top of his right foot from the warming pan.

Matthew roughly sheathed his knife and strode across the room. “Is that it?”

“What do you mean, is that it? The pan is still in the bed and filled with red hot embers,” Myles retorted, still nursing his injured foot.

Matthew rolled his eyes, then shook his head. “All that bloody commotion because your beds overly warm!”

Myles, in no mood for Matthew’s comments, waved his arm towards the door. “Now you are satisfied I am not in mortal peril, get out. Go on!”

Matthew, grumbling under his breath, left, shutting the door loudly when he did.

The redness had begun to subside, and the pain had, he admitted, been more the shock of finding the unexpected hot pan between the sheets rather than the physical injury. Still, that was no reason for Matthew to treat his outburst as childish. If it had been his feet, he was sure the man would have acted no differently.

Myles was about to rise and remove the offending pan from the bed when there was a knock at the door.

“Go away, Matthew,” Myles said bluntly.

The knock repeated.

Realising it probably wasn’t Matthew, the bald man would have admitted himself after his first knock, he rose and limped towards the door. Hauling it open he found Susie on the other side, who jumped back in fright.

"Ah, it's you," Myles said, stepping back, "You're too late, I found the warming pan."

"I'm sorry, Master Devereux, I was comin' to take it out when Master Matthew sent me to get him some supper," Susie said quickly.

"Did he, indeed. Well come in and take it away," Myles stepped to the side to allow Susie into the room, eyeing her distrustfully, "And I thought you'd left it there out of spite!"

Susie didn't reply, but reddened slightly under his gaze. "Did you burn your feet?"

"Just one," Myles admitted.

"There'll be a lesson for you there, then," Susie replied, carrying the pan towards the door.

Before he had the chance to reply she'd gone leaving Myles staring at the closed door. How dare she!

Chapter 6

By the morning, his headache had subsided, but Devereux's sour mood had not. He slept late and was woken by Matthew's impatient tap on the door. A moment later, his head appeared around it, and he announced. "Uttridge is here."

Myles, still surrounded by linen sheets, scowled at Matthew.

"And what do you want me to do about Wignot. He's in the taproom, ready to plead on his knees before you," Matthew added.

The reminder of the previous evening did not improve his mood. "Send him away. He lost in front of a dozen witnesses. Send some men over to secure it. It seems we now have a tannery."

"It seems so," Matthew said. He sounded about as impressed as Susie had the previous night.

Myles waved his hand towards Matthew. "Out. Go on. I'll call for Uttridge when I'm ready."

As it happened, Uttridge was a man he did want to see. His lawyer was organising the purchase of Slouch's shop. Swinging his legs from the bed, his eyes searched the carpet for his slippers, which were always neatly placed near the head of the bed.

But not this morning.

Bare feet on the cool carpets, Myles found his bedrobe was not on its hook near the fire. Instead, it had been left draped over the back of his desk chair near the open window. The fur was damp and jewelled, with a fine drizzle, the wind had blown through the window during the night. Myles pulled the cold robe around his shoulders, grimaced when the cold, wet fur caressed his neck and began a hunt for his slippers. Amica was watching him from the warmth of the bed he had just vacated.

"Don't look at me like that, you ungrateful creature," Myles said, raising the covers draped over the edge of the four-poster bed and peering beneath; still no slippers. They were also not by the fire, in any cupboards, or apparent beneath his desk. What had the damned woman done with them? The fire was out; he'd not even bothered to try and rekindle some life into it the previous night; there was little he could have done with wet wood clad with swollen moss.

Myles gave up the hunt; wrapping the robe tightly around himself, he pulled the door open. "Get that Harrington woman up here, now."

"I thought you wanted Uttridge?" Matthew said, slightly confused, from where he was perched on the end of a coffer.

"Harrington first, if you please," Myles said through gritted teeth before retreating into his room.

Looking as defiant as she had the night before Susie Harrington arrived.

"Pray tell, woman, where are my bed shoes?" Myles growled.

Susie said not a word, rounding the bed to the opposite side she leaned down and produced them from under the edge of the bed.

"I'm sure you find this amusing," Myles said. Snatching them from her hands he dropped them to the floor and slid his feet inside.

"I'm not sure what you mean, Master Devereux," Susie said, her eyes on the floor.

"Yes you do. Wet logs in the basket, a fire that wouldn't keep a rabbit warm, my bed robe left to be soaked near the window, and my bed shoes hidden out of sight, not to mention the scalding bed you left for me last night!" Myles finished.

"I'm sorry, master Devereux, I was busy in the tavern last night if yer recall, serving the men, I'd not the time to see to your room properly," Susie said in the same neutral tone.

"Just get out. Take that wet wood with you and have more sent up. Go on, out," Myles said waving his hands towards the wood basket next to the fire, she didn't look at him as she collected the wood basket and left.

Myles followed her to the door. "Send Uttridge up, now."

A few minutes later, Uttridge arrived and hurried through the open door to Myle's private rooms. An efficient and brisk man, he arrived with the papers he needed fastened inside a leather case tied closed with legal ribbon.

"Well?" Myles said. His feet were beginning to warm up, but his mood was still as cold and damp as his bed cloak.

"Kemp wants to keep Slouch's house, but he is happy to sell the workshop to you for the amount you offered. He also has Slouch's ledger which, as I pointed out to him should, by rights, go with the business, and he has affirmed he will have one of his servants deliver it," Uttridge finished.

"Why doesn't he want to part with the house?" Myles asked.

"He feels there may be a profit from that he could make himself. A botchers shop isn't of any use to him, but a roomed property that he could rent would be a different proposition," Uttridge replied, laying a leather filed on the desk and unfastening the ribbons. "I have the paperwork here to complete the transfer."

"Kemp didn't ask for more?" Myles said, an annoyed note in his voice.

Uttridge shook his head. "No, Master Devereux, he didn't."

"I knew I should have offered him less," Myles said, stalking across the room, the long bed robe trailing behind him.

Uttridge wisely didn't say anything, but continued to organise his papers.

"Anything else?" Myles said, peering at the vellum sheets over Uttridge's shoulder.

"Can I please ask you to append your signature, here and here ..." Uttridge tapped the pages he had laid on Devereux's desk.

Myles pushed the sleeve of the bed robe up, exposing a naked arm printed with gooseflesh. He found a pen, dipped it, and added his signature to the two sheets in quick flourishes: 'MD.'

Uttridge poured pounce from a small pouch onto the two documents, shook it to dry the ink, and then blew it from the pages. It clouded in the air around Devereux.

"Do you mind?" Myles said, annoyed.

Uttridge flushed. "I am sorry, Master Devereux."

"Everyone is today. If any questions arise over the transaction, bring them to me," Myles said, watching Uttridge fit the signed sheets back into the leather case and wrap the legal ribbon around the tabs holding it closed.

"Everything has a price, has he not told you what he wants for Slouch's house? My wish is to own them both," Myles said.

"I feel this may not be the issue," Uttridge smiled, "There is a situation Kemp is about to find himself in that he is unaware of, if you would allow me to outline this I think you will be quite happy, and also able to place a lower offer for the property when it comes available, as I am sure it will."

Myles sat back down in his chair and folded his arms. "Go on then, Master Lawyer, entertain me."

Uttridge cleared his throat and began. When he had finished Myles had been more than entertained, for once he found himself having a genuine appreciation for his lawyer. When Uttridge left he was replaced by Matthew.

"Well, do you have a botchers shop and a tannery now?" Matthew said.

Myles ignoring the reference to the previous evening said. "We need someone to oversee Slouch's shop."

He'd need to appoint someone to oversee Old Slouch's business. Peggy Delwyn he needed to run it, at least for the moment, but she'd had too much freedom with Slouch's business. That wouldn't be the same now Devereux was in charge.

"Good. I told you not to leave that woman in charge, you'll have trouble mark my words," Matthew said, his thumbs finding his belt.

"Indeed. So who should we send?" Myles asked.

"You mean one of my men?" Matthew's eyes were wide.

"Actually, one of mine, but I shall set the issue of possession aside for the moment. So yes, one of the men," Myles said, his dark eyes fixed on Matthew.

Matthew strode across the room. "Well, whoever you choose, you can tell them. None will be pleased to be given the job of watching over a roomful of harping women. After all, they are your men."

Myles looked towards the ceiling. "You are not viewing this very well, are you? It's a good post. Indoors, there's a fire and food, and nothing more dangerous to deal with than the sharp edge of Peggy's tongue. I would have thought there would be a queue for such a job?"

"That's what you might think, but they'll take it as a slight, mark my words," Matthew said.

"I care not a jot for their pride, Matthew. Who would say is the most able?" Myles asked.

Matthew shrugged and then said quickly. "And don't look at me, either. I'm not spending my days surrounded by harridans and stinking piss pits."

"I wasn't thinking of sending you, but if you don't start being a bit more bloody helpful I will," Myles growled in reply, "Who do you suggest?"

Matthew's brow creased in thought for a moment. "Probably Jasper Cutlake. He's got an easy manner, not likely to lose his temper, and he's looking to prove himself. He might not like the task, but he'll do it well."

"Good, well, get him sent there then. And you can go with him and ensure Mistress Delwyn knows he is in charge," Myles said.

"You tell him yourself!" Matthew shot back, then added, "and while you're at it, why not send that Haddington woman over there now that you're finally fed up with her?"

The rest of Myles' morning continued to not go to plan. Two hours later, he was at the tannery he had won at cards, accompanied by Matthew and his men.

The rope had stretched under the weight of the body. Danny Wignot's toes, hanging from slack ankles, grazed the dusty floor of the tannery. Behind the suspended body was a fallen stool, used no doubt by the tanner to loop the rope over the roof beam before wrapping it around his neck and taking his final plunge. It was a drop of no more than a few feet, not enough to have snapped the man's neck despite his weight. And the contortions of his final moments were etched still on his face. Snot had run from his nose, snagging in his beard and dangling like winter icicles beneath his chin. Purple and impossibly swollen, Wignot's tongue protruded from this mouth, ringed by his thick, dark lips. It was a tongue Myles did not want to look at, the memory of when he'd bitten it was one he wanted to banish from his mind forever.

Worse than all of this were the eyes.

Wide open and bloodshot, they engaged immediately with anyone entering the door to the tannery, their gaze unwavering and accusing.

Standing beside Devereux, thumbs secure in his belt, Matthew said, "I told you he was a sight."

Myles, his head slightly towards one side, regarded Wignot critically, a look of disgust on his face. "It's an inconvenience, to be sure."

Matthew grunted. "More than that! What do we do with him?"

"What do you mean, do with him? Report his demise and then have him cut down," Myles replied.

"You will be blamed for this, and probably rightly so," Matthew growled in his ear.

Myles turned on Matthew. "I did not force the wretch to take a fatal step into the air."

"Maybe not. He came to the Hart to plead with you, and you wouldn't see him, and now he's dead. You took his business from him. Don't you think that looks a little suspicious?" Matthew's words were tinged with anger.

Myles shook his head and pointed a long finger towards Danny. "You had to have the last bloody word."

"I'll send a man to inform the Justice," Matthew said.

Myles continued to look at the tanner. Danny Wignot, alive, hadn't been an attractive man, but dead, he now resembled a mason's gargoyle. Myles eyes couldn't help themselves but rest on the extended tongue, a tongue not that long ago that he had sunk his teeth into so hard he'd filled not only Danny's mouth with blood but his own. His stomach churned at the memory.

Damn Wignot!

Matthew returned and began pulling on his riding gloves. "It's time we were not here."

"Does it matter?" Myles said, in no mood for another scolding from Matthew.

"It does. The sheriff is going to want to fix the blame for this somewhere, and I'd rather it didn't get hammered on our door," Matthew said, signalling to his men that they were to leave as well.

"It won't. The tavern was filled with witnesses, Matthew; if you remember goading him on to risk all at cards, it wasn't my doing. Danny Wignot is hanging there now due to a very unhealthy mixture of greed and idiocy," Myles pointed to where the tanner hung from the roof.

"That might be so. But being elsewhere when the justice arrives would be wise, unless you want to watch while they cut him down. See the final event play out," Matthew said sarcastically.

"What exactly do you mean by that?" Myles said turning on Matthew.

"You killed him. He might have taken that last step by himself, but it was you who placed him on that stool with a noose around his neck," Matthew said, an arm pointed towards the dead man.

Myles, slightly taken aback, glanced between Matthew and Danny. "Since when did your chest begin to burn with humanist principals?"

"It doesn't. It was an act that was bad for business. Men will trust you less now. They know you are not a fool, you duped Wignot, and they know that. So the question they'll be asking themselves is who'll be next?" Matthew said bluntly.

"I've had enough of your prattling, Matthew," Myles said, turning his back on Danny as he stepped from the tannery and back into the windy street outside.

When Myles returned, he was annoyed to find that Richard Fitzwarren had managed to get the better of his men. He was sitting in Myles' room in a chair by the fire, awaiting his return, Amica happily purring in his lap.

Myles had known Fitzwarren for a long time, too long. He was a ruthless mercenary, and if tales he heard were correct, very much in demand. Fitzwarren's, cool, self-assured eyes ran over Myles, a half-smile on his face. Myles was pleased to note he had not missed the gloves.

"So, Fitzwarren, you're back?" Myles began slowly pulling the ruby gloves from his hands.

"A fairly pointless observation," Fitzwarren replied, then pointing towards the gloves. "A gift?"

Myles laughed. "Indeed a gift."

Fitzwarren raised an eyebrow. "There's hope here yet! You have an admirer?"

"A gift from myself," Myles corrected.

Fitzwarren shook his head. "There really is no end to your self-obsession, is there?"

Myles ignored the comment, asking instead, "Why are you here?"

Fitzwarren's smiled broadened. "Civility mostly. I had a care to see how you were faring given recent events."

"Recent events?" Myles repeated, wondering suddenly if Fitzwarren was aware of Tasker's sudden disappearance after he had made an attempt to take over Devereux's business.

"I hear there's been a change of ownership at the Black Swan Tavern," Fitzwarren said.

Myles suppressed a scowl. How Fitzwarren knew about that, he didn't know and Myles disliked anyone taking an interest in his dealings.

As if Fitzwarren had read his thoughts he said, "I only know because I recently frequented the Swan. Your choice of landlord did surprise me, however."

"Why is that?" Myles said, failing to keep the annoyance from his voice.

"Tongues will wag, he's taking great pains to style himself as you," Fitzwarren replied.

A genuine smile lit Myles' face and he laughed. "Perhaps in appearance, but certainly not in wit. He knows his place, don't you worry about that."

"I wasn't .... and what do we have here ...." Fitzwarren had risen from the chair and reached towards the bedpost. Wrapping his hand around the hilt of the sword that rested there, he lifted the blade.

"You saw that the moment you stepped through the door," Myles said, pleased all the same that Fitzwarren was holding the weapon. "Hard to miss when you placed it there on display," Fitzwarren said, his eyes on the blade he held before him. "That's Norfolk's coat of arms."

"You are right. I'll gift it to Matthew in time, he has his eye on it," Myles replied.

"I'm sure he does. It's a fine piece," Fitzwarren ran the fingers of his right hand down part of the runnel on the blade. "It's filthy, you should take more care of it. So who's blood is it?"

"No one you would know, but he's no longer a problem," Myles said with satisfaction.

"I can see that. The blade went in up to around here, he was wearing a leather jacket, and I'd say he was taller than you by a good foot, and he met his end just in front of where you are standing now." Fitzwarren observed.

Myles stared at Fitzwarren. "Any more guesses you want to make?"

"Not guesses, the blood's run down the runnel quickly before the blade was pulled free, so the strike had to be upwards. The blade was pulled out of the body before the blood made its way to the hilt. It was turned point down .... " Fitzwarren pointed the blade towards the floor before Myles. "Your carpet has been badly cleaned. Then, after you'd slain your assassin, you put the blade back here, reversing the direction of the blood, which ran down to the tip and left a second stain on your carpet just about there," Fitzwarren dropped the tip of the blade onto a small brown stain near the foot of the bed.

"Very good," Myles said sarcastically, clapping his hands slowly.

Fitzwarren held up his hand. "I'm not finished. The blade went right the way through, piercing his back, hence the stain on your carpet, he landed on his back .... "

".... How do you know!"

"Simple, he had to have been within striking distance, and there's not enough space for him to have fallen forwards and, now I am guessing, here, but I don't even think you would drive a blade through a man's back," Fitzwarren announced, then picking up the blade again he brandished it towards Myles. "He was also a fool, and slow witted."

"How can you know that?" Myles said, his temper rising.

"Easily. He was not similarly armed. There's not enough space in this room for sword play, and he was too close to you, so you took him by surprise. I'd lay a healthy wager the blade was already resting here. So you had the advantage of surprise and, luckily, a weapon that bridged the gap between you," Fitzwarren said.

"Meaning?"

"Meaning, you could strike before he could lay a hand on you. Such a direct thrust with a sword would have been easily deflected by anyone with a degree of skill with a blade, so he was not a man trained to fight with one. Indeed, few are," Fitzwarren raised the sword again, this time offering the hilt to Myles.

Myles hesitated for a moment before wrapping his hand around the leather bound hilt and holding the sword out level.

"One of the first things you learn is how to disarm your opponent. A man without a weapon is a far easier kill than one holding ...."

The pain in his wrist was the first thing Myles was aware of before his hand opened and the blade was knocked from his grasp, the quillons rattled against a coffer lid and the pointed end of the blade snagged in the carpet.

"What the Devil was that for?" Myles snarled, retreating, a hand wrapped around the injured wrist.

"Sorry?" Fitzwarren said.

"Sorry! You nearly broke my bloody wrist!" Myles spat back.

Fitzwarren stooped, retrieved the sword, and propped it back against the bedpost. "You bested a half-wit, don't believe you can wield that against anyone who has ever had any training."

"A lesson! You arrogant cur!" Myles growled.

"It's been said," Fitzwarren said, "Near enough everyone who holds a sword had one pressed into their hands when they were a child, it becomes instinct, don't think you can equal their skill."

Anger flushed Myles' cheeks and he rounded the other side of the desk, putting the solid oak between him and the other man.

"Settle your temper, Myles, you know I'm right," Fitzwarren said, scooping Amica from a chair he sat down, the cat on his lap.

"Words would have been sufficient," Myles said sullenly.

"You forget. I know you quite well," Fitzwarren said, then addressing the cat, he continued, "your Master is hot-tempered at the best of times and stubborn beyond belief at the worst."

"Harsh," Myles said.

"But true, and anyway Andrew would be less than pleased if I had failed to deliver an adequate warning," Fitzwarren replied, his dark cool eyes meeting Myles'.

"Damn you," Myles said, "That was unfair."

"Indeed," Fitzwarren said, his eyes still on the cat, "But, the warning has been adequately, if somewhat bluntly, delivered."

Fitzwarren's tone was apologetic, and Myles, cursing under his breath, rounded the desk and took the chair opposite.

"Let not arrogance and ignorance be your undoing," Fitzwarren said meeting Myles' gaze.

"I could surprise you, I might learn to wield one," Myles replied sulkily.

"As I said earlier, most men with any skill have held one before they lose their milk teeth, so it's a little late, and I don't want you to meet a man as good as my brother, and speaking of family, how is my father?" Fitzwarren said changing the subject.

"You duped me, Fitzwarren, you knew he was an ailing man. A dead lord is not a lot of use, is he," Myles said.

Fitzwarren, still smoothing down the cat's jet-black fur, rested his head back against the chair and met Myles' gaze. "So, he's still alive. I'm sure you profited well for bringing him back from London, and continue to do so to ensure his security."

Myles, ignoring the truth of Fitzwarren's words, said, "He's a dying man, and you failed to mention that fact."

"We are all dying men, Devereux," Fitzwarren said.

"And your brother, Robert, attempted to bring a charge of habeas corpus, accusing me of keeping the old shit against his will. You owe me for that; lawyers' fees don't come cheap, you know," Myles said and had the satisfaction of seeing Fitzwarren's eyes snap up from where they had rested on the cat - he'd not been aware of the writ it seemed.

"I presented your father, and the proceedings were dismissed," Myles said, "an inconvenience and an expensive one."

"I am sure you have billed my father sufficiently to cover your expenses. It would be very unlikely for you not to use such an occasion to turn a profit," Fitzwarren said, smiling.

Myles scowled at the accuracy of the statement and said, "He's an interest in your blond brother, though. Shame he's taken such a dislike to you, that would have been the easier path to wealth."

"It's not mine to take. Sometimes, life is not just about how full your coffers are," Fitzwarren said.

"Don't preach, Fitzwarren, we both know it's a short and damnable life when they are empty," Myles retorted.

"True. I see you've still got your cat. Amica, if I remember correctly," Fitzwarren said. "It's a start."

"What now? More lessons!"

Fitzwarren smiled. "Find another stray. And speaking of the future, did you sell the Astrologica?"

"Is that why you are here?" Myles said, his eyes narrowing.

"No, I was providing you with a change of subject matter, if you must know. Accept it, and I apologise for the lesson. So, do you still have it?" Fitzwarren said.

"I do. It was, as you said, a little hard to sell, and it has had its uses." Myles failed to hide a smile as he remembered when he'd shown it to Tasker and purported to cast his horoscope.

Fitzwarren's eyes narrowed, a smile twitching the corner of his mouth, amused he asked. "Who have you been entertaining?"

"No one of note. It still holds my curiosity. You told me John Dee had one, and he knows how it works?" Myles replied evasively.

"I did. I am happy it has captured your interest," Fitzwarren sounded genuinely pleased.

"You told me you know Dee. Can he explain the workings?" Myles asked.

"I'm sure he could, but that's not to say he will. Dee is .... difficult on occasion," Fitzwarren replied.

"You are difficult regularly," Myles shot back.

Fitzwarren grinned. "I shall see if I can broach an introduction. Have you ever heard where it came from?"

Myles shook his head.

"Unusual, I am sure it is being missed by someone. I don't think it would be wise to show it even to Dee," Fitzwarren said, his voice serious once again.

Myles nodded slowly. "If he has one, and he wishes to explain the workings to me, tell him I will pay."

Fitzwarren nodded. "He takes payment for horoscopes, so I may be able to add you to his client list."

"Very well, and what do you think of this?" Myles lifted a gold goblet from his desk, the metal cold in his hand, it was the one he had discarded on the floor of the taproom.

"I had noticed that. Have you become, like an infant, drawn to shiny objects?" Fitzwarren asked.

"We are all drawn to gold," Myles offered the goblet, and Fitzwarren, detaching a hand from Amica, accepted it.

"Weighty," Fitzwarren said, hefting it in his hand, then running his thumb over the rubies that decorated the stem. He added, "They appear to be real rather than glass. It has some age, I would guess. There are signs of use, and," he reversed it to examine the base, "I would say it was French in origin, and probably dates to the time of French King Charles VIII."

"Why do you say that?" Myles asked, frowning.

"The base is broad and flat, and the stem quite short; the fashion changed to a taller, more elegant style when Charles had a set made for his coronation. After that trinkets like this tend to be taller and set on a slimmer base."

"It's hardly a trinket!" Myles said.

Fitzwarren looked up from the goblet, his dark eyes meeting Myles'. "We both know this was filched from an altar, so what else can it be? If you like it, then enjoy it, but you can't trade it, or even show it off. Our current monarch would take a very dim view of you having possession of it."

Myles hesitated for a moment before turning and opening a cupboard. Inside was a small portable altar, the leaves folded closed. He retrieved it and set it on the desk, his long fingers opening the wooden doors to reveal a central panel with the virgin and, on either side, saints, haloed and kneeling, flanking her.

Fitzwarren gently placed Amica on the floor and rose. "Is this wise?"

"Probably not, but it is about to be a shared problem," Myles' mouth twisted into a smile.

Fitzwarren regarded him with a cool stare. "Why would that be?"

"I recently came into possession of quite a lot of it, and as you have pointed out, keeping it here was unwise," Myles said carefully closing the panelled wooden doors.

Fitzwarren's face hardened. "Perhaps you had better show me."

"Certainly, it's at your father's house," Myles said, smiling broadly.

"What did Fitzwarren suggest?" Matthew asked after Fitzwarren had left.

Myles scowled. "That I smelt a portion and see what the Jewish smiths will give me for it."

Matthew shrugged. "It's good advice, and the same as I gave you if you recall."

"Alright," Myles said, picking up the goblet from his desk and examining it with a sad expression. "Very well, have it reduced into something anonymous, and I will find out what it can be sold for."

Matthew smiled, and immediately relieved Myles of the goblet. "Good, I will do that now. It is a wise decision."

Myles watched him leave. Not at all convinced that the decision was a wise one.

Chapter 7

Ultimately, it was a trade, and Myles and Matthew were happy. Matthew informed Susie where she would be working and took her to the botchers shop, where Peggy Delwyn had been delighted by the provision of an extra pair of hands. Myles dealt with Cutlake.

Cutlake had been working for Devereux for just over a year; he was on the fringes of the dozen who accompanied Myles whenever he left the White Hart; he'd stood in for Parry Dutton when the idiot man had sliced his hand open with a knife trying to prise open an oyster. Myles was aware of his efficient manner, his eagerness to take Devereux's horse when he was finished with it, the way he sat straight backed and attentive in the saddle. He had a poise and a bearing many of the men didn't, and it was through his own easy manner and likeable character that they didn't resent him for it either.

Jasper Cutlake had trained as a knight, endured a hard and demanding upbringing and then lost it all in a moment. Cutlake had been in a roadside tavern, there for no other reason than taking a meal on a break from a journey back to his father's estates in Wiltshire.

An argument had broken out in the tavern; why and who was to blame, he couldn't have known, but the odds were not in the favour of the one man who was being beaten by half a dozen assailants. Cutlake, young and armed with the righteousness of his calling, waded in to defend the downed man, a stool in one hand and a poniard in the other. The fight had been short, and he had delivered a good number of numbing blows with the stool, dispersing the aggressors quickly. The rest of the tavern had shrunk back and looked on silently. There had been no cheer of appreciation from the drinkers for his heroic intervention, and the downed man had escaped at speed through the kitchens at the back of the Inn.

Cutlake had seen the looks of horror on the faces of those in the tavern and realised he had made a terrible mistake. The man that had darted from the back of the tavern was Mace Black, wanted for the rape and murder of Christian Heron, the daughter of Simon Heron, miller. He had been recognised by one of the groups who attacked him who had called his name, and Black had raised his head, confirming his identity. Realising he was trapped, he had made to run for the door but had been stopped, and the men had begun to deliver justice to him on the floor of the tavern before Cutlake freed him.

The crime Black had committed had been horrific. An assault against God and poor

Cutlake was now all they had to strike at for vengeance. And they did. Despite his pleas, and despite the provision of a lawyer by his father, he was tried as an accomplice to Black's crime. It was a falsehood. And recognised by many as such. But the allegations had been made, Cutlake was in gaol, and set to be tried for a crime that by rights should have been faced by the now disappeared Mace Black.

The sheriff realised quickly enough that time would allow the wronged family to see sense, and Cutlake had languished in gaol for six months. Luckily for him, Mace Black was found. Cutlake was tried for affray, convicted, fined and released. But his association with Black would not be forgotten in a hurry, and his father wisely did not want Cutlake back. Instead, he had approached Matthew and handed his son into his employ. His father knew no reputable house would take Jasper, but Matthew, whose employer lacked such scruples, would.

Matthew had taken him, and if Myles was honest, he was pleased to have amongst his men one who had noble ties and knightly training. He saw Cutlake as something of a prize, and in time he would become a very visible part of Devereux's dozen, there just needed to be an opening, and to date none of the feckless fools had got themselves killed so he was very much waiting for dead men's shoes. But it was just a matter of time.

Working for Devereux was an employment that carried with it a degree of risk.

Cutlake was a good choice, and none of the other men would feel he had been singled out for a particularly good task, either.

Matthew tapped on the door an instant before his head appeared round it. “Cutlake is here.”

Myles placed his palms on the edge of his desk and was about to rise when he changed his mind. “Send him in.”

Matthew frowned, but did as he was bid and a moment later Jasper Cutlake stepped through the door. If there was any man amongst all of Devereux’s that he could ever see raising a challenge to his leadership it would be Cutlake. Myles swallowed and tried to banish the vision his mind had just created for him. One of Cutlake dressed by Master Drew, an altogether more formidable image than the one Devereux was. He had no reason to suspect that this was Cutlake’s ambition, but he could take over Devereux’s role; he had the presence of mind, the intelligence and more than that, he would create an image that would overshadow Devereux’s. Cutlake was about Myles’s own height and age, but that was where the similarity ended. The torso beneath the plain but immaculate doublet told of a lifetime of practice at arms. His neck was thick and muscled, and the backs of his ungloved hands wore the fine white tracks of healed wounds. Short, neat hair was capped with a bonnet set at an angle, and beneath that, a handsome face with a neatly trimmed beard.

"Master Devereux, you sent for me?" Cutlake said in his smooth, well-rounded voice.

"I've work for you, Cutlake," Myles said.

"I am, as always, at your service," Cutlake said, with a degree of sincerity that actually made the listener feel like he meant it.

"I've a new business acquisition, you may have heard about it," Myles said.

Cutlake grinned. "The tannery, I would guess, sir."

A moment of annoyed confusion flittered across Myles' face. "No, not that. The botchers shop, it was owned by Slouch, he died some weeks back and it's now mine. It does not have a master in place at the moment and is being run by a woman called Peggy Delwyn, and I would like you to oversee it."

"Oversee it?" Cutlake repeated the words slowly.

"Yes, I want to know everything about how it works, and I want records keeping of the income and expenditure, I want the money that comes through the shop recorded and brought here, and I don't want any of it sliding into Peggy Delwyn's hands, do you understand me?" Myles said.

"I do indeed. You want me to ensure your new business is running to make you a profit," Cutlake said, not sounding at all annoyed that he was being deployed to a botchers shop full of women.

“Good and that woman from the kitchens in the Hart, Susie, she is to go to work there as well as they are short of hands, so take her with you,” Myles added.

“You can count on me, Master Devereux,” Cutlake said bowing.

“Good,” Myles waved a hand towards the door and a moment later Cutlake was gone. Myles would find out soon enough whether or not he’d made a good decision.

Chapter 8

Uttridge, following Myles' orders, ensured the priest, Kemp, was aware that retaining possession of Eldridge Slouch's house was a folly. The sale of the shop was not in contention, but the Priest knew the value of property in London, and he was reluctant to part with Slouch's house. He recognised the good rent that could be claimed for the property year on year and was unwilling to be cheated out of it by Myles Devereux, so while the sale of the botchers shop wasn't an issue, the house was.

Uttridge was aware of the cleric's desire to retain what he believed to be his, however that wasn't going to happen, and his position of authority was being bolstered by the presence of one of Devereux's more capable men, Cutlake, who was propping up the wall, arms folded across his chest and regarding the cleric with a cool stare. "I am afraid, it's an issue of access that is causing a problem."

Kemp, who had already heard Uttridge's argument several times regarding the lack of access to Slouch's house was present at the botchers shop, the bequeathed keys in his hand and eager to quash any issues pertaining to access.

Uttridge, his worn leather folder under his right arm, stepped through the front door of the botchers shop, nodded to Mistress Delwyn, and moved to one side to allow the priest to enter.

"As you can see from the front, there is just the one door, and if anyone were to access the house they would first need to traverse through the botchers shop here," Uttridge said, indicating the six or so feet between the front door and the one that led to Slouch's house.

"It's a few feet. Surely, Master Devereux can have no objection to someone crossing his threshold to get to that door. It is not as if they would be wandering around his workshop?" Kemp said in consternation, waving an arm towards the door.

"It's more than a few feet," Cutlake said, pointing towards the gap in question. "More like six."

Kemp rolled his eyes. "Very well, five or six feet, I grant you that. However, it is no more than two paces from the front of the building to the door of the house. How can there possibly be any objection to that? The area is not used for anything else, anyone entering the house would not need to go into Master Devereux's property."

"If only it were that simple," Uttridge lamented, shaking his head and adopting a saddened expression.

"It is simply, you legal dolt, two steps," Kemp said, his temper rising.

Cutlake pushed himself away from the wall and rose to his full height to stand behind Uttridge. "Now, sir, there is no need to call into question Master Uttridge's profession. I would remind you that he is Master Devereux's representative on this matter."

"But this is ridiculous, I wish only to use this doorway so a tenant can be found," Kemp continued.

"Indeed. What if the shop is locked, then how does a man access the house? Should he have keys to the workshop, could he be trusted to lock the outer door behind him? Is he a trustworthy soul?" Uttridge said pleasantly, wondering just how long it was going to take Kemp to realise that trying to retain a hold on Slouch's house was pointless.

"This is ridiculous, Uttridge. From what I can see all that would be needed would be a short corridor here with two doors one on the left for the workshop and one on the right for the house. That's all, then it would have separate access, and there would be no need for anyone to trespass anywhere, would there?" Kemp complained.

"That would be a solution, and I can see how your mind would leap to it. But you cannot build a corridor here or place a doorway there without impinging on land owned by Master Devereux," Uttridge explained, enjoying himself immensely, he pronounced. "I am afraid, sir, it is a matter of easements."

"A matter of easements," Kemp repeated, his brow furrowed, and he bestowed an unkind look on Uttridge.

"Indeed. What is at the heart of the matter here are the easements. That right to pass and repass through this very doorway is governed by the law of property. For you to be able to access the door to the house formerly owned by Master Slouch you would need to take, one .... two.... three steps," Uttirdge entered the doorway and stepped towards the door.

"So?" Kemp spat the word.

"Sir, to do so you would require an easement, a right if you wish, to use this small area for the single purpose of traversing from the door threshold here to the doorway over there. It matters not to the law whether it be three steps or three miles, the legality of the matter remains the same," Uttridge said, then to Cutlake, "Wouldn't you agree?"

Cutlake's brow furrowed and he nodded sagely. "I am not a legal man, Master Uttridge, however, what you say makes sense, and if it is the law of the land, then it must apply here, and it makes sense that it makes little difference if the distance is a short or a long one."

Uttridge smiled. "Exactly my point."

"So, what are you saying is that I just need an easement?" Kemp said, now sounding confused.

"Indeed," replied Uttridge, as if that was the point they had been in search of for some time.

"At last. This easement, I can obtain one?" Kemp said, sounding relieved.

"Of course, it would be a simple matter of having the right drafted in a legal document and from then on you can pass and repass as you and your agents wish," Uttridge provided.

"And I apply for this how? Via the court perhaps?" Kemp ventured.

"Alas no," Uttridge replied, again his visage adopting a saddened expression.

"How then, man?" the irate and legally baffled priest demanded.

"Well, sir," Uttridge continued, ignoring the priest's rising agitation, "you would need to petition the property owner for the easement."

"The owner of the property," Kemp said slowly.

Uttridge smiled broadly. "Exactly. Master Devereux."

"But I sold it to him! You supervised the sale?" Kemp shot back.

"Indeed I did, and you were happy with the terms, if I recall. Master Devereux's consideration for the shop was generous," Uttridge replied.

"Why didn't you tell me then that the sale would lead to this ridiculous state of affairs? Where I cannot gain access to property left in the bequest?" Kemp fumed.

Uttridge adopted a sad expression, but his eyes were as hard as flint. "I work for Master Devereux, not you."

Sudden understanding blossomed on Kemp's face. "It's a matter of money, I see. I have the keys to Slouch's house; it may be that there is access at the rear, and then I won't need to be bound by the ties of your master."

Uttridge shrugged, and both he and Cutlake followed the priest as he selected a key and presented it to the lock in the door to Eldridge's house. Uttridge continued to wait patiently while three more keys were tried, until finally the last one turned the lock.

As the door opened the men were hit instantly by the sour odour from inside. Intense, eye-watering and identifiable as the stench of death.

"Did they remove him?" Uttridge said, gagging and stepping away from the door, his hand over his mouth.

"God's bones," Cutlake gasped.

"They did! Unless I committed an empty shroud to the earth," Kemp gasped. "Perhaps he had an animal, a dog, that has been trapped within?"

"Maybe," Cutlake said, not sounding at all convinced.

"I do not think this is wise," Uttridge said, his hand over his mouth, as he followed Kemp over the threshold. The smell worsened as soon as they entered, and their movement in the narrow passageway had disturbed several dozen fat black flies.

Uttridge retreated immediately. "I think this may be a matter for the justice."

Kemp looked him squarely in the face. "I think you might be right. It may be that another crime has been committed."

All three men retreated, the outer door to Slouch's home was closed, and a boy was sent to bring Justice Daytrew.

Daytrew was an hour in arriving. Kemp was becoming increasingly impatient and his mood was poor when Daytrew finally made an appearance. Uttridge had sent his own assistant to a bakeshop for food and was licking his fingers of grease when Daytrew and his retinue finally arrived.

"You've kept us waiting, Daytrew," Kemp said, advancing on the justice; it was obvious he believed that he outranked Daytrew.

The litter was set on its spindly legs and two men placed the step stored on the back next to the opening. Daytrew, ignoring the priest, swivelled his bulk on the seat, the litter swaying dangerously on the supports, one of the men at the back lent his weight to the wooden frame to keep it upright. Daytrew's legs emerged first from the litter, his gown riding up around his knees. Wriggling forward, he transferred his weight to his feet and squeezed from the litter. Rearranging his gown and cloak around him, he stood on the top step and looked down at the priest with a look of contempt.

"Come on, man, get down here," Kemp said, gesturing with his arm towards the botchers shop. I've a meeting with the bishop this afternoon; I can't wait all day."

Daytrew, disregarding the priest's chiding words, descended the two steps and took a final long stride to avoid the puddle of muck in the street, which put him on the drier stones outside the botchers shop. He was followed by two of his men who had ridden behind the litter and handed the reins of their horses to the litter bearers.

"What seems to be the problem?" Justice Daytrew addressed Uttridge, rather than the priest.

"Death is the issue, sir," Uttridge replied.

"A body has been found?" Daytrew said, sounding instantly excited, then added, "there was no such mention in the message sent to me? Is it murder?"

Uttridge shook his head. "We've not found a body, as such."

"What do you mean, as such?" Daytrew shot back.

"There's a smell, and we think ...." the priest interrupted.

Daytrew's eyes widened. "You brought me here because of a smell?"

"A smell?" Myles drawled stepping up behind Daytrew and making him jump.

"Master Devereux," Daytrew stammered.

"Indeed," Myles said in agreement, smiling at the priest and the justice.

"Why are you here?" Daytrew asked.

Myles shrugged. "Curiosity mainly. Uttridge had the sense to send me a message after you were called for. So, tell me more about this mysterious stench."

"I've nothing to tell, sir. I have just arrived," Daytrew said defensively.

Myles looked mildly upset. "Well then, man, investigate!"

"Yes, quite," Daytrew said, turning back to Uttridge. "Where is this odour? Are you really sure it is a matter for a justice to be dealing with?"

Kemp, who still had the keys, stepped forward, unlocked the door again, pulled it open, and, with a kerchief over his mouth, stepped to one side. This allowed the full force of the noxious odour to roll towards Daytrew and Devereux, along with a dozen black flies that buzzed their way into the daylight. Uttridge and Cutlake had the sense to move to the street away from the open door.

Daytrew flung a sleeve across his mouth, and Myles backed quickly into the street, no longer as curious as he had been a moment ago.

"Unless that is the smell of a rotten butcher's shop, I think we can assume there are remains in there," Kemp said.

"It could be a dog. Has nobody been to check?" Daytrew said from behind his sleeve.

"We were waiting for you," Kemp said, then pointing towards the doorway, "Go on then, man."

Daytrew, a man used to taking an order when given one made to step forwards towards the open door, and then stopped and retreated, directing his words towards his own men. "You two, in there, and find out what ails the air."

Two of Daytrew's men, looking decidedly unhappy about the task, each took a large lungful of fresh air and quickly entered Slouch's house. One went upstairs, and the other took the lower floor.

There wasn't much to it. Downstairs a kitchen, and room with a fire where Slouch had taken his meals, then upstairs two bedrooms. The one where Slouch had been found dead and another that he had taken to using for storing anything he thought of worth.

Myles could hear the men's feet stomping quickly back towards the door. Both men emerged at almost the same time, happy to be back outside in the cleaner air of the street.

"Well, what did you find?" Daytrew demanded.

"There's nothing upstairs, the rooms are empty, save for a bed," the man who had emerged first replied.

And the one who had been on his heels said, "Nothing downstairs either."

"Did you check cupboards and coffers? You weren't in there very long," Daytrew reprimanded.

"There's none to check upstairs, Justice Daytrew, only the bed, and there's nothing under it, I looked," one of them replied.

"It's open shelves in the kitchen, nowhere for there to be anything hidden, Justice Daytrew. Maybe the smell is from the river," the second man added helpfully.

"It can create a proper stink at the banks, especially if it's near a tanner or butcher's yard," the other chimed in.

"We are not near enough to the river here," Daytrew said.

"There's a brook runs along the back. Eldridge used it for washing his rags," Myles said helpfully, then added, "It runs beneath the house, and if it is obstructed, it could be to blame."

Kemp looked at Devereux, then back at Daytrew. "You need to investigate, sir. You cannot trust the words of your men, they were hardly in there long enough to find anything ."

At that moment a woman's voice, and one Devereux recognised said, "good to see you again sir. Can I help?"

Myles turned to see Peggy, a basket over her arm and a net bag hanging from her shoulder filled with squat round loaves.

"Mistress Delwyn," Myles announced, fairly sure that neither the priest nor Daytrew would be pleased with the woman's appearance, so he continued. "There appears to be a rather terrible odour coming from Master Slouch's home, it is almost as if he's not left. Justice Daytrew's men can find nothing that could be the cause. Do you think it could be the brook?"

"Justice Daytrew's men might have found something had they taken the time to look," Kemp said accusingly.

Peggy laughed. "Years of piss, lye an' rags 'ave left me wi' little sense o' smell. A kindness of the Lord, if you ask me. Let me get rid of the bread an' I'll go in and air it out for you. A few open windows and it'll be not so bad."

Peggy disappeared with her burden of bread, and the men waited for her to return in the wake of this sensible suggestion. When she did, her hands empty of basket and bags, her sleeves pushed up to her elbows as usual, she bustled past them, pulled open the door to Master Slouch's house and closed it behind her. All three of them could hear her wooden shoes on the steps and floorboards as she moved around the house from room to room. After a short while she emerged, propping the door open.

"The windows are all open at the back, an' there's a fair breeze blowing so it'll take the smell out in a few minutes, sir," Peggy said to Master Devereux.

"What would Justice Daytrew have done without you?" Myles said happily, then added to the further annoyance of the justice. "You should thank Mistress Delwyn."

Daytrew's eyes went from Devereux to Peggy, and his fat lips compressed into a thick slug at the bottom of his face. He had, it appeared, little intention of even acknowledging her presence, let alone speaking to her.

"Aye, well. If you'll excuse me, Master Devereux, I've lassies the to see to," Peggy said, ignoring the priest and Daytrew, and with her head high and hips swinging, she headed back into the botchers shop.

"Hideous woman!" Kemp muttered, watching her retreat.

"But at least she has cleared the way, so to speak, for Justice Daytrew to investigate," Myles said.

"Indeed. Daytrew are you going to, then. The air has cleared," Kemp said.

Daytrew, not about to be ordered around by the priest, said to his men, "In you go again. The stench has been removed. See what you can find and report back here."

They were gone this time for much longer, but when they emerged they had nothing more to tell the justice, the house was empty save a few furnishings, and there was nothing to account for the smell.

Myles, tiring of the proceedings, took it upon himself to be the next through the door.

"Master Devereux," Daytrew called from behind him. "I really should insist on being the first to enter."

"You didn't seem overly keen," Myles threw back over his shoulder as he made his way into the house. He wasn't overly interested in where the stench was emanating from, his interest was purely in the building which he was hoping to acquire for very little. Downstairs were two good-sized rooms, one with a fire, and a kitchen towards the back of the house. Daytrew followed him through each of the rooms. There was, as his men had said, very little to see. The kitchen was narrow, on one side were simple open shelves against the wall, at the end a cooking fire, and light entered from a window high up on the opposite wall to the shelves. The smell, also had retreated.

Myles headed up the steep stairs, careful to keep his gloves from the dusty banister and his sleeves away from the walls which also threatened to soil his doublet. There were two rooms, one to the left and another to the right of the stairs. Both the doors were open, and the one to the right could be seen in its entirety, it was empty, the one to the left held the bed where Eldridge had been found dead. And it was into this room that Myles stepped. The evil odour that had rolled out of the front door to greet them was still present despite the shutters having been flung open.

Myles heard footsteps on the stairs again. It was Peggy.

"There's nowt 'ere Master Devereux. I think it was the smell of death from when poor Master Eldridge died that had got locked in."

Daytrew joined them in the room, his nose wrinkling in distaste. "As my men have already said, there is nothing here."

Myles wasn't listening. Something was here.

A single fly buzzed before him, hovered for a moment uncertainly, then flew upwards.

Myles' eyes followed it as it headed towards the smoke darkened ceiling. The beams were alive with black flies, and more were gathered around the edges of the open window. A muted rustling emanating from the bed met his ears and was gone as quickly.

".... If yer want to come down, I can show yer the back of the workshops where the brook runs; that might be the cause of this, I suppose ...." Peggy was saying to Justice Daytrew.

"Shhhh ...." Myles, raising his hand.

".... Like I said I canna smell a thing these days, robbed I've been of ...."

"Shhhh ...." Myles tried again, stepping towards the sound.

".... It's been a blessing, mind. The best lye is made with the strongest piss you can get, and I can remember on St Agatha's Saints Day, bless her soul, with the sun pouring heat from the sky, the stench was ...."

"Will you still your tongue, woman," Myles commanded.

Peggy stopped talking, but her shoes drummed on the bare boards as she backed from the room, and several more flies, dislodged by the noise, flew up and criss-crossed the room.

Myles pointed a long finger at her. "Mistress Delwyn, your silence, and if you please, don't move."

The woman stopped. Shock on her face. "I'm sorry Master Dev ...." Realising she'd spoken again, she slapped a hand over her mouth and backed into the door slamming it into the wall.

Myles rolled his eyes at this final cacophony of noise and shook his head. Whatever he had heard had ceased. Maybe it had come from outside the window; crossing to the open shutters, he leaned out. Below was the brook, and outside was cleaner air; the room was the worst for the smell. Turning back, Myles looked at the bed. It was nowhere near as grand as his own. A sturdy box design which would have provided enough space for Master Eldridge and, when he had one, a wife. The footboard was edged with a scalloped design, and below it, lines of punch holes had been imprinted to form the shape of a flower. In the centre of the footboard, well carved and interlaced were the letters E and M.

"What was his wife called?" Myles asked the room in general.

"Maud .... Master Devereux," Peggy said, eager to please, "She died years ago, a fever. It's often the way, and poor Master Eldridge ..."

"Enough," Myles raised his hand again, then to Daytrew, "Are your men downstairs?"

Daytrew nodded.

"Call them up," Myles instructed.

"I'm sure there's no need, what is it you want, Master Devereux," Peggy said, clomping back into the room.

"I want this bed turning on its side," Myles said.

"I don't think that's right and fitting, poor Master Eldrige has 'ardly been out of it," Peggy wailed, clearly upset.

"Woman, get downstairs. Go out, this is men's business," Kemp said harshly.

Daytrew scowled at the screeching woman, adding, "Get gone."

Peggy could be heard crying and clomping loudly down the stairs.

Daytrew cursed under his breath and waddled to the top of the stairs, calling down for his men to join him.

"Tip it on its side," Daytrew commanded, pointing towards the bed.

The men exchanged confused glances.

"You don't employ on the basis of wit, do you Daytrew?" Myles said, then to his men, "Lift it onto its side, we wish to view the bottom."

One of the men shrugged and joining his companion they fastened their hands around the edge of the frame and began to lift the bed. The mattress was still in place, deep and linen bound, and a sheet was still tucked in neatly to the bed frame. The bed was solid, oak and made to last. The two men raised it the level of their knees and halted, adjusting their holds before raising it the level of their chest.

Myles, Daytrew and Kemp watched as the bed was hauled up over. Beneath the white linen sheet, a bulge began to emerge, as they raised the bed, pressing hard against the sheet. A sudden stain appeared in the middle of the taught linen, dark and spreading from one end to the other, the smell that had met them at the door assaulted their nostrils once more, and as if released from a cage, the room was suddenly filled with the black bodies of angry flies.

"Good Lord!" Daytrew gagged, his hands over his mouth.

A crucifix was in his hand, and the priest took a step back. "Tis a devil!"

Myles moved towards the sanctuary of the open window as the men made their final groaning efforts and raised the bed to the vertical, ejecting from the middle of the mattress a body that rolled, rotten and tangled in the linen sheet to the floor.

"And that, Justice Daytrew," Myles said pointing towards the source of the smell, "is your problem."

Chapter 9

As soon as he returned to the White Hart Myles discarded his clothes, he was sure the corpses reek had come with him, the noxious odour seemed to linger on him still. By the time he reached the top of the stairs his cloak was unclipped and when he was two steps inside the room it shed from his shoulders to the floor. His fingers were now intent on the task of unfastening the doublet as quickly as possible, paying little heed to the precious buttons as he tugged them loose.

Matthew opened the door, his face creased with confusion, and saw Myles hauling his arms from Drew's latest creation and dropping it to the floor.

"Get someone up here and get those cleaned," Myles announced, a long finger stabbing the air in the direction of the abandoned clothing.

"What are you doing?" Matthew's gaze switched between the pile of saturnine clothing and the man, who now wore only a shirt and hose.

"Trying to rid myself of the stench of a body. Christ Matthew, Davey Langton did you a bloody favour by making you go to the Swan market today," Myles said; stripped to his linen shirt, he hauled the door to his room open.

"What body?" Matthew said, following him in.

Myles, his head now inside the linen was pulling the shirt from him, his voice, muffled. "In Slouch's house."

"I don't understand? Why were you at Slouch's?" Matthew said, his red leather bonnet in one hand and the other scratching at his flattened hair.

Myles bundled the shirt into a ball and jettisoned it into the outer room before dropping into a chair and beginning to pull his boots off. "Uttridge met with that damned greedy priest, Kemp, and Cutlake, wisely, sent a message to me to attend after they opened Slouch's house and were met with the stench of death."

"Was it Slouch's body?" Matthew stepped sideways to avoid one of Myles' boots that he slung across the room.

Myles shook his head. "I've no idea whose body it was. I doubt it was Slouch. Even the priest confirmed he'd seen his corpse in a shroud."

"So who was it?" Matthew asked, his arms flung wide.

"Good question," Myles said, tugging the second boot away from his foot; looking up at Matthew, he said, "It was inside the bloody bed, pushed inside the mattress. Daytrew's men upended the bed and the putrid thing rolled out."

"It was rotten?"

"Chokingly so. The smell, the flies. It's been there some time," Myles replied, shuddering.

"Inside the bed? How?" Matthew quizzed.

"Someone must have cut the mattress open, pulled out the straw and wool and repacked it with an altogether more horrible filling," Myles said, "There was a linen cloth still on the bed covering the abomination, so it had been hidden there on purpose."

"Could it have been there when Slouch lay dead in his bed?" Matthew's eyes were widening.

"Who knows? Perhaps, bloody stupid place to hide a corpse, don't you think?" Myles dumped the boot on the floor, rose and began to loosen the ties on his hose. Once they were removed, they followed the shirt out of the room through the door, and Myles, naked, wrapped himself in his bed robe before slamming the door shut.

"Does this mean Slouch has been murdered?" Matthew continued.

Myles grimaced. "I'd not thought of that, but I suppose so."

Myles slopped wine from a decanter into a glass, a quantity escaping over the rim to pool on the floor. Raising the glass, he sluiced the liquid down his throat before refilling it a second time.

Matthew shook his head with a slight smile as he watched the younger man. "I didn't think a bag of bones would rattle your nerves."

Myles emptied the glass and turned on Matthew. "My nerves, Matthew, are intact, finely strung and in good order. However, the assault on my nose and person was less than pleasant."

"For Lord's sake, man, it was just a stench! When did that ever do harm to anyone?" Matthew scoffed.

Myles waggled the empty glass in the air before Matthew. "Say what you like, you weren't there. Indeed, I've a good mind to send you there so you can share the unwanted experience."

"So Slouch could have been murdered in his bed then?" Matthew shook his head.

"Perhaps. It's a little hard to tell now that he's been buried," Myles said, then added. "If he was, then we are never likely to know."

"Or did Slouch himself hide the body?" Matthew said, tugging at his beard as he considered this.

"What? And he vanquished his assailant, stuffed him in a mattress, covered it with a neat linen sheet and then climbed into bed on top and expired after a heart attack brought on by the effort?" Myles said sarcastically, then waving his glass towards Matthew, said, "No doubt Daytrew will come to that conclusion."

"So it must have been hidden there after Slouch died?" Matthew pondered.

"It's a fair assumption, the house is empty. It's been left to the church, and his chattels were disposed of .... apart from the bed," Myles drummed his fingers on the table. "I think that's quite significant, don't you?"

Confusion clouded Matthew's face. "I'm not sure what you mean?"

"The bed! Matthew, think. A bed is about the most valuable piece of furniture a man owns; it's often specifically left in a final testament to a friend or relative. It has a value."

"Oh, and you'd know how much beds are worth," Matthew said, jerking a thumb in the direction of the monstrous four-poster that dominated the room.

"I shall ignore that comment," Myles said cooly, before he continued, "and here is Slouch's bed, the only item of furniture that's not been stripped from the house, and I think we know why."

Matthew grimaced. "So whoever emptied the house knew the body was there?"

"Or indeed, put it there," Myles set the empty glass down and pulled the bed robe tight around his body.

Matthew spread his arms wide, confusion on his face. "Why leave a body inside a mattress? It's going to be found sooner or later."

"True. And it's bloody inconvenient," Myles said.

"Why?" Matthew said slowly.

"Well, if Daytrew deems it a murder, he'll be spending his time there over the next few weeks, you know what the fool is like. I was hoping to buy the house and have the deal done within the week," Myles complained.

"Whose going to want to buy it after a rotten corpse was found in it," Matthew shuddered.

Myles' brow furrowed. "Good point, I shall have to revise my offer."

Matthew shook his head, and Myles grinned.

More details of the incident arrived quickly. Uttridge, attended by his scribe and puffing from the exertion of the journey from Slouch's, arrived at the White Hart an hour later. Myles was still swathed in his fur bed robe when Matthew admitted the red-faced lawyer to his room.

"Well, is that shit, Daytrew, going to get in my way?" Myles asked his lawyer.

"Probably," Uttridge said, then added. "There is little I can do at the moment to further your cause to acquire the property, not while Justice Daytrew is investigating what has happened to the woman we discovered there today."

"Woman?" Myles said, his brow furrowing.

Uttridge nodded grimly. "It seems so, the flesh was so putrid it wasn't immediately obvious, but it has been confirmed as female, and it seems Slouch's servant is missing. The Delwyn woman has said as much."

Myles leaned back in his chair and regarded Uttridge over his steepled fingers. "And what is Daytrew making of this tangled corpse?"

Uttridge shrugged. "If foul deeds have been committed then no doubt the sheriff's inquest will uncover them."

Myles pinned Uttridge with a cold stare. "You are not in a court room now. There is no need to curb your thoughts. Entertain my curiosity, man."

"It would be usual to hold an inquest where the body is found. However, because the body is so putrefied there is concern that it could unbalance the humors of those attending the proceedings in such a small space, so they are not going to hold an inquest at Slouch's," Uttridge replied.

Myles laughed and slapped a palm on the table top, and wrinkled his nose. "I doubt the sheriff and the coroner would wish to be confined with the hapless victim for overly long. So what are they proposing to do?"

"The body was removed and taken to Swain's boatyard," Uttridge shuddered, "the physician, Master Drake, instructed it to be sent there and sluiced with river water to remove the worst of the putrefaction, and it's being kept under water out of reach of the flies and rats until tomorrow when he will review the injuries."

Myles' eyebrows rose. "Injuries?"

"It seems so, what they are I cannot say, but Master Drake, when he fleetingly viewed the corpse, said there were killing wounds to be seen," Uttridge provided.

"Killing wounds?" Myles repeated. "What did he see?"

Uttridge spread his hands wide. "I am afraid I cannot say, sir. I was outside of Slouch's house with your man, Cutlake, when the physician arrived after Justice Daytrew summoned him. All I know, Master Devereux, is that when he emerged from Slouch's house, he told Daytrew that this was a matter for the sherrif and that the corpse had evidence of 'killing wounds.' His words, sir, but more than that, he did not say."

"Hmmm. And Daytrew, what news of London's chief idiot?" Myles asked, folding his arms.

"He has been asking questions, and he has men posted at Slouch's house, and also at Swains boatyard," Uttridge said, then added. "Your man Cutlake, a good man by all accounts, has asked me to request that Master Matthew send over some more men to support him given that the justice's men are there now as well."

Myles looked towards Matthew. "See to it. I'll not be seen as being outnumbered by

Daytrew. If Daytrew's men are charging curious Londoner's a penny to view the house again I want to know about it."

"I think that will not happen this time," Uttridge reassured.

"Daytrew is a fool; don't be so sure that he'd not continue to choose men who will dupe him. You might like to think that Daytrew has more sense, but the workings of the justice's mind would be a mystery even to God," Myles said, then losing interest he added, "let me know when the coroner will be making a verdict. As soon as the matter is away then we can press on with acquiring Slouch's house. Go on, be off with you."

Uttridge, relieved to be dismissed, bowed and made a rapid exit through the door.

As soon as it closed Matthew turned on Myles. "You want me to send men to guard a rag house? I'm sure Cutlake can manage to control a half dozen women and some slop pots!"

"I'll not be seen to be outnumbered?" Myles shot back.

"Oh, right then. But it's alright though for London to think you've gone mad guarding a bloody woman's wash house," Matthew said.

"They can think what they damn well like, and when your men are there tell Cutlake I want to talk to him," Myles said.

"Men's tongues are going to wag over this. Mark my words! Devereux needs a dozen men to keep his scolds in line, you'll be a laughing stock!" Matthew crammed his leather bonnet back on his head.

"Just do it," Myles said with finality.

Cutlake was admitted to Devereux's room two hours later, and Myles' mood took another turn for the worse. Cutlake, clean, well-clothed, every inch a man of his station, cut a finer figure than Myles, who was still cowled in his bed robe. Myles was acutely aware of this. He seated himself behind his desk, pulling the robe closed. At least Cutlake couldn't see his bare feet.

Cutlake presented Myles with Slouch's ledger book. "One of Kemp's men dropped this in earlier in the week."

"The churl, he was supposed to send that here, not the to the botchers," Myles grumbled.

Amica, impressed with the new arrival, was winding her way between Cutlake's boots.

Cutlake smiled at the cat, then to Devereux he asked. "May I?"

Devereux rolled his eyes. "Why not, everyone who enters this room seems ever more enamoured with the mouser."

Cutlake straightened, the cat now cradled in his arms, Amica on her back, paws poised, letting him scratch her chest. "I gave my sister, God, rest her soul, a kitten very much like your cat."

"It's not my cat. It's the tavern mouser that's strayed again," Myles said, annoyed. He glared at the cat, willing it to extend its claws and dig them into the back of Cutlake's hand. But Amica, relaxed and purring, was enjoying the attention. "What do you make of the incident at Slouch's today?"

Cutlake looked up from Amica. "A curious event. I've not had an inkling while I have been there that such an evil act had been committed, nothing of the like has been hinted at by the women."

"What have you learnt since you've been there," Myles asked.

"Since Slouch died, as you know, Peggy Delwyn has been in charge," Cutlake began lowering the cat gently back to the floor. "Old Slouch had allowed her to run the shop, pay the women, strike deals with the merchants and collect in dues from buyers. She was supposed to pass all of this to Slouch for him to record in his ledgers," Cutlake paused and prodded the ledger with a forefinger decorated with a solid-looking gold band. "Now, Slouch got lazy. In the last few months, he'd not left his rooms much due to ill health and relied more and more on Peggy. He even allowed her to keep an amount back to pay the girls, each received a loaf a day from Pattey's bakery and then a payment at the end of each week. Now I believe, although none of it can be proved, you understand, that Peggy probably hasn't passed all of the money she collected to Slouch."

"And why do you think that?" Myles' eyes narrowed, and he leaned forward across the desk.

"Because since his death and when I arrived, there has been no income from the shop. Peggy argued it's all been spent on payments to the bakers and the girls and that they've sold very little, but I am very sure it's a lie," Cutlake said. "There should have been some money from the date Slouch died to when you sent me to oversee the shop surely? It can't be that the money spent and the income balance exactly so there is nothing left to record?"

"When did the entries in the ledger stop?" Myles pulled the book towards him and flipped through the pages to the last entry.

"It is hard to say, Master Devereux, I have looked at Master Slouch's ledger, but it is woefully short of dates, as you can see for yourself," Cutlake said, "And the first dozen pages have been so wet the ink has run and it's illegible."

As Myles flicked back through the pages, he could see that Cutlake was annoyingly correct. There was no way to tell when the entries had been made.

Cutlake pointed towards the last page. "Those final entries are my own. They relate to money paid to the bakery and money received from several buyers. I've listed them all there, and this ...." Cutlake fished inside his doublet and produced a small purse. "Is the balance."

Myles took it and tipped the contents, primarily poor coins, onto the desk.

"As you say, there should have been more," Myles commented, his eyes on the groats and half pennies. After half an hour with Cutlake, Myles realised he had sent the right person to oversee the botchers shop. Cutlake had taken to his task seriously and enthusiastically.

Chapter 10

Matthew rapped on his door and a moment later his head appeared. "The woman you wanted is here."

Myles picked up Slouch's tattered ledger and made his way to the outer room.

Mistress Delwyn, a broad smile on her wide face, bobbed a curtsey. "Master Devereux, how can I 'elp. Yer man, 'ere, said there's an issue of a confusion?"

Matthew scowled at the woman. "I said nothing of the sort! I said Master Devereux had some questions."

"Thank you, Matthew." Myles raised his hand, then to Peggy. "Slouch recorded his dealings in this ledger, but without the mind of the man who wrote it, his accountings are a little hard to interpret."

Peggy looked confused.

"For example, he doesn't say which of the entries relate to customers and which relate to his expenses," Myles said.

"Master Devereux, I'm not sure I can 'elp yer. I wish I could, but I've not the reading, and that just looks to me like a jumble of crow prints in the muck," Peggy said, pointing a rough-skinned forefinger towards the open pages in the book Devereux held.

"I'm not asking for you to read it," Myles opened the ledger and raised it so he could read it, finding the point where the ink was still legible. "Here we have the name Cartright? Whose that?

Peggy's eyes brightened. "Jess Cartright brung in rags and Master Slouch bought them from 'im. He's a travelling type, a seller of buttons and ribbons, travelled outside London and he brings in sacks of rags to sell."

Myles nodded. "Regularly?"

"Three or maybe four times a year he'd come. The lassies loved it; he'd always 'ave some bits of ribbon for them," Peggy said, grinning.

"Indeed," Myles said impatiently and took a pen and placed a mark next to the name. Seller.

"Next is 'bread' – there are dozens of entries for this," Myles asked.

"Aye, well, there would be; the lasses are paid in bread and coin, a loaf a day and a coin at the end of the week. Master Slouch always used Pattey's, the bakers in the next street," Peggy said nodding and folding her arms across her chest.

Myles nodded. That explanation took care of a lot of the entries. "Hackton? Who's that?"

"Mistress Hackton owns the laundry down the street from Pattey's. Her husband died, Lord rest 'is soul, the year old king Hal, God rot him, died and ...."

"Yes, but why is she in the book?" Myles stabbed the page impatiently, this was going to take all day.

"As I were tellin' you, Master Devereux, Mistress Hackton has the laundry now. By way of her business cloth comes to her that's no use, or it doesn't get collected, an' she needs to get her money back o'course an' then she brings it to Master Slouch ...."

"She's a seller then?" Myles interrupted impatiently.

"Yes, sir, she is," Peggy said, sounding a little hurt.

Myles opened his mouth about to tell her exactly how little he cared for Mistress Bloody Hackton and her inheritance when a voice in his mind he recognised chided him.

"Your impatience will cost you, Devereux," Fitzarren had said laughing.

Myles found his purse, selected a coin and held it up between them, smiling he said. "Mistress Delwyn, your time is valuable, how about we play a one word game? I'll give you the name and you can just say to me buyer or seller? If Slouch paid them for anything then they are a seller and if he received money from them then they are a buyer. Is that clear?"

Peggy's eyes were on the coin. "Yes, Master Devereux."

"So just say, buyer or seller. And this ...." Myles twisted the coin between his fingers, ".... Is yours. Right – Pickwick?"

"Ah now, he's got ...."

"The game …."

"Seller," Mistress Delwyn said nodding.

"Brintyn?" Myles said, his pen hovering near the next name.

"Buyer."

"Prentice?"

"Seller."

The process went on swiftly for two more pages. Myles placing a mark next to each name, some were now being repeated so the pages were quicker to check.

"Harrington," Myles said, coming to a new name.

Mistress Delwyn hesitated for a moment.

"Buyer or seller," Myles asked, looking up at her from the book.

"Seller," Mistress Delwyn said firmly.

Myles looked at the next notation in the column, it said, "and son."

"What does this mean? He's written below Harrington 'and son'?" Myles asked.

Mistress Delwyn's mouth remained firmly closed. Realising why Myles said, "It's alright the game has stopped for a moment, you can tell me."

"He was Master Haddington's son, Master Slouch paid the father and sometimes the son worked as well," Mistress Delwyn provided.

Myles marked the book next to both names and moved to the next one. "Muncyn White?"

"Buyer."

"Barton Finsbrook?"

"Buyer."

"Maddy Crinlock?"

"Seller."

"Finney?"

"Seller."

After another six pages they had completed the book.

"Since Slouch died you've had to pay for bread from the bakery, is that right?" Myles asked, watching Peggy carefully.

Peggy nodded. "Aye, sir, Pattey's bakery, same one as we've been using for years. Bread is always fresh and unlike that thieving devil in Canning Road, he cut's his flour with dust. It's been said that if you're a stranger he'll sell you bread that's good enough to make stool legs from it's got that much wood dust in it. Mind you I would ....."

"Mistress Delwyn, please!" Myles exclaimed, exasperated.

"Aye, sir, sorry sir," Peggy said, biting her lip.

"Where did the money come from to pay Pattey's or did Slouch run an account?" Myles asked.

Peggy shook her head. "I pay when I collect. Master Slouch always paid up front, good and proper with good coin."

Myles nodded. "And buyers. Surely you've had a few since your poor Master died?"

"Aye, we have the usuals, and it was the market last week so that always brings a few in as well," Peggy confirmed. "They'll go see what's for sale on the market and then come to us an' see if we' ave anything cheaper."

"Good, that makes sense. And normally you'd give this money to Master Slouch, is that right?" Myles asked.

Peggy shook her head. "Master Slouch always dealt with customers, they'd go into his rooms and he'd make a mark in that book you've got there."

"Ah, of course," Myles said, "And he'd then give you the money for the bakery?"

"That's right Master Devereux, and I'd go an collect the bread for the lassies," Peggy confirmed.

"But what about since Master Slouch died? Whose taken the money from the customers?" Myles asked, his dark eyes fixed on Peggy's face.

She faltered. "Well, some of it I tooked and .... Well there weren't much .... And I paid it all over the bakery."

"All of it?" Myles said, "I thought the lassies, you said were paid at the end of the week?"

"Oh, yes an' that of course," Peggy said quickly.

Myles flipped the book to the blank pages. "And none of that is in here?"

"Course not Master Devereux, I cannot write. An I swear on all that is holy, Master Devereux, that I've only paid the bakery and the lassies, with what little there was."

"I am sure you did," Myles said, in a tone which conveyed very clearly that he was positive that she hadn't.

"Can I go now, Master Devereux?" Peggy said, her voice jangling with nerves.

"Indeed, and all money will be handled from now on by my man Cutlake," Myles said.

Peggy smiled. "Oh aye, the lassies are all fallin' over themselves having such a man about the place."

"What do you mean 'such a man,'" Myles said coldly.

"Yer just need to look at 'im with a woman's eyes. He's as bonnie as heather on the hill, that one. There'll be a long line of lassies wanting to tie themselves to that lad, I can tell you. And charm! The girls hardly ever hear a kind word, and like hens, he's got them eating grit from his hands," Peggy said, relieved with the change in subject.

"Has he indeed," Myles said coldly.

Peggy received her coin and left, and Myles now had a book marked up that he could use to work out the profit Slouch had made from his botchers shop, it was simple task of totalling the income and spend. As they had moved on through the book the process had become much easier, Myles recognising names that repeated and knowing now that they were sellers or buyers with no need to ask Mistress Delwyn. His feeling was that Slouch had made a good profit, and that keeping the shop going in more or less it's current fashion would be profitable enough.

Myles seated himself behind his desk, and began to make totals at the bottom of each of Slouch's pages one for the money coming in and the other for money going out. Each page satisfyingly showed a profit, with more income than expenses. He'd even found his own name in Slouch's writing on the occasions when his men had delivered shrouds to the shop for disposal. He'd been paid a relative pittance for them, Slouch knew nowhere else would take them, and Myles had no doubt he had made a good profit from them. With a little more investigation of Slouch's journal he had no doubt he'd find a name with the notation 'buyer' next to it that would have been acquiring them from Slouch. Myles frowned, annoyed with himself, if he'd asked Mistress Delwyn he would, he had no doubt have been provided with a lengthy and detailed explanation of who bought them and how often. Knowing would not help him, Slouch was dead, and the past was a sealed vault.

The botchers shop would not make a fortune, but it was a regular income, and it gave him a useful business in a street which was satisfyingly close to Bennett's territory and once he secured the house then he could find some way to profit from it. He could rent it, expand the workshop, use it as storage or even open another business in it. It was an opportunity, and Myles Devereux was never one ignore one.

Myles stopped in the act of reaching for a glass.

Haddington.

Leaning across the desk he pulled Slouch's journal towards him, flipping rapidly through the pages. He stopped when he found what he wanted.

'Haddington – a shilling.' Then his mark indicating he was a seller.

Myles dog eared the page and began to work backward in the ledger slowly, his finger running down the lists, he found the name four more times, then in the section where the ink was blurred he was sure the name Harrington was there. There were no more mentions of the name in the final dozen pages of the book.

What made the whole document so annoying was that Slouch had not entered a single date from the beginning of his accounting to the very end. Myles guessed the end of the entries coincided with his death, but when the start was wasn't clear. It might be that there was a date on the first page, but that had suffered the worst in terms of water damage and none of the text was legible, all of it had run to become just a black swirling stain on the page.

Myles pulled a candle closer, and began to work through the ledger again, not looking this time a the names but instead searching for a clue as to the dates. There was none. What use was a bloody ledger without a date! Myles fumed.

Master Harrington and his son. Both paid by Eldridge Slouch regularly it seemed. Myles dog eared each page where the name appeared. Then they stopped, he leafed forward another dozen or so pages, checking again, but the name Harrington did not appear.

Myles drummed his fingers on the desk.

He dealt with Slouch three of four times a year. Springing from his chair Myles retrieved his current account book and began flipping the pages until he found the last receipt from Slouch.

Slouch – 2s 3d

Slouch – 4s 6d

Slouch – 9s 4d

It was slow work, but Myles enjoyed a puzzle. Very soon he'd matched the amount of 2s 3d to Slouch's records and his own ledger provided a date nearly two years ago. It was ten pages before the last entry for Haddington, and Myles had to retrieve another ledger from the coffer, Haddington appeared at the top of the page, and half a dozen lines below this was another payment he could match to his ledger, and the date he could give to this was February 11th of the previous year, a little over 18 months ago.

When had Susie said her husband and son went missing?

Myles pushed the ledger from him. It proved nothing. Haddington wasn't an uncommon name, and so what if he'd worked for Slouch, it meant nothing.
beneath his corpse had been hidden the murdered remains of his maid. The hollowed out remains, if Uttridge was to be believed.

Myles sat back in his chair. What was he doing? He had no idea at all if this was Susie Haddington's husband and son, and if it was what good was it? He'd left her, taken his son and finding his name, if it was his name in a ledger proved what? He could very well have worked for Slouch before he left his wife. It meant nothing. Myles pushed the ledger from him – why was he bothering with the affairs of a woman who had treated him with such spite recently?

A grin spread across his face. She was at the botchers now. A few weeks up to her elbows in piss and working at the White Hart and being allowed to clean his room would look like living in a palace. Women needed to be reminded of their place, harsh words were insufficient, they were too thick skinned a breed to heed them. But a few weeks in Peggy Delwyn's company would give her a good measure of his displeasure.

Chapter 11

Matthew knocked on the door a moment before his head appeared around it. "Uttridge is here."

Myles, a pen in his hand, his bed robe around his shoulders, as yet had not dressed for the day. He waved his hand towards Matthew. "An hour."

"He wished me to impress upon you that there was some urgency attached to his visit," Matthew said.

"What is it with bloody lawyers! Their dealings always require urgency, but when you wish for them to act for you, they dawdle like infants," Myles complained.

Matthew's expression hardened, ignoring Myles' complaint he said, "He's outside, and his concern should be ours as well, he'll not speak his mind to me. Today was the date set for the inquest into the body at Slouch's, remember."

Myles discarded the pen. "Oh very well."

Matthew disappeared, and a very pale Uttridge entered the room. Myles frowned; the file was no longer clamped beneath his arm, and his hat was slightly askew.

"What requires so much haste, Master lawyer?" Myles said, leaning back in his chair.

"The coroner, Master Devereux .... the proceedings were this morning, I have come straight here with the news," Uttridge stammered.

Myles rolled his eyes. "Foul play was already suspected. So why is there a need for this intrusion?"

Uttridge swallowed. "It was the nature of the crime; the physician had examined the remains but not pronounced his findings until this morning."

"Well, he wouldn't, would he? What gossip has paled you like milk and ruined my leisure?" Myles continued.

"It does appear that the body is Mistress Marnie Dobbes, she was Slouch's maid-servant. The physician, Master Drake, believes she lost her life at around the same time as Slouch died, and has been in the house since then," Uttridge said, clearly appalled at the crime.

"That makes sense. So?"

"The murder was most foul, Master Devereux. He cannot for certain say what the cause of the good ladies demise was, on account of the advanced state of decay, but there are parts .... missing," Uttridge paused, "I was at the inquest, it was most horrible."

"If you remember, I, too, was subject to the reek of death. If you've come here to tell me you have a weak stomach and that the rats had enjoyed a pleasant feast, then get out," Myles said, waving a hand towards the door.

Uttridge shook his head. "Not the rats, Master Devereux. Master Drake showed the jurors and the coroner where the insides should have been, and the poor woman's ribs had been sliced through from neck to stomach."

Myles' eyes widened. "Proof of murder, then?"

"I would think so, Master Devereux," Uttridge replied. "And there was nothing inside the cave of her chest, she'd been left hollow."

"Hollow?" Myles repeated, sitting a little straighter in his chair, his full attention now on the lawyer.

Uttridge nodded slowly. "The physician, Master Drake, holds that everything above her stomach had been cut away and pulled out."

"Could it not have been rats? A body is a fine feast," Myles asked.

"There were knife marks inside her on the ribs near her spine," Uttridge paled further. "Master Drake pulled away some of the ribs to show the coroner, and they were passed to the jurors; the cuts were not the gnaw marks left by vermin," Uttridge finished, shuddering.

Myles shook his head. "Old Daytrew'll be agog now, what's the idiot make of it?"

Uttridge's fingers had found the fur trim at the front of his robe and were clasping it in his sweating hands. "That's why I made such haste, Master Devereux, to warn you, sir."

"Warn me?" Myles said, confusion clouding his face.

Uttridge nodded. "Justice Daytrew will be here soon."

"Why?"

"They feel there may be a connection, Master Devereux," Uttridge said with obvious reluctance.

"A connection? For the Lord's sake, man, spit it out?" Myles demanded, his palms on the desk, he rose from the chair.

"It is known you wished to buy Slouch's business," Uttridge said weakly.

"Only because the shit was dead," Myles shot back.

"I feel that might be the point they are focussing upon," Uttridge said reluctantly, his voice a quiet whisper.

Silence fell like a cold, wet blanket on the room. It was Matthew who broke it. "And did they allege this at the inquest?"

Uttridge shook his head. "Not in as many words, Master Matthew. But the coroner has requested that Justice Daytrew also inquire into the nature of Master Slouch's death as well, as this now cannot be ruled as natural and owing only to God."

"Slouch has been in the ground for over a week, what are they proposing to do?" Myles said.

Uttridge swallowed hard. "The coroner has requested that his body be examined for murder marks. His passing on to the next world was confirmed only by the priest, Kemp, and at the time it was thought only that his demise was attributed to his age, and that it was his time to be called to God. But now they are not so sure."

"What are they going to do? Dig up his rotting remains?" Myles said incredulously.

Uttridge didn't reply, but the look on his face was answer enough.

"My God!"

"Indeed," Uttridge accepted.

"What can they hope to learn?" Matthew interrupted.

Uttridge turned towards Matthew. "The concern, after finding this poor creatures earthly remains, is that something similar may have happened to Master Slouch, the priest is not a medical man, he didn't summon the justice when the death was reported, so it is felt much could have been overlooked."

Myles shook his head. "And how is Daytrew faring in all of this?"

Uttridge smiled, here at least he could provide some good news. "Not well. The implication is that there is much that he has missed. The death was reported, but Daytrew paid it no heed, and, in his own words, treated it as 'an old man's passing.' The coroner was very scathing at this point, you of course know that he too is a man of advancing years and pointed out to the justice that murder was not a plight suffered only by the young."

"Perhaps it will occur to them to rid themselves of the incompetent fool," Myles scoffed.

Matthew stepped forwards. "If you hear any more, please bring the news straight to Master Devereux. When do they propose to dig up old Slouch?"

"Before sunset, was the suggestion from the coroner, so I would imagine that the poor old man's eternal rest has already been broken," Uttridge said sadly.

Matthew and Myles exchanged a quick glance. The grave diggers at St Bride's were men provided by Myles and paid for by the parish, and Thomas Cleggston, Myles' man, was in charge of them.

Matthew, a hand on Uttridge's elbow, began to steer him towards the door.

"You know how to be in the wrong places, don't you?" Matthew fumed when the door was closed and Uttridge had been dismissed.

"What do you mean?" Myles erupted from his chair, the fur robe shedding from his shoulders.

Matthew swiped the bonnet from his head and slapped it down with a solid crack on the desk. "I heard Uttridge! Look where your bloody ambition has got you now! You could never stand Slouch making money that you couldn't."

Myles stared at Matthew, his eyes wide with disbelief. "And why is that such an issue? Slouch made money from rags, it was a profit I couldn't make, so why shouldn't I have been unhappy about it? And he paid less than he should have, we both know that."

Matthew's face boiled with temper, he snatched the leather hat and waved it in Myles' face. "Greed! It'll be your bloody undoing!"

Myles just stared at him. "I am not responsible for this crime, damn you!"

"I didn't say you were. What I said, is that your bloody greed has placed us at a disadvantage again," Matthew waved his arm towards the door. "It'll take more than Uttridge's assurances to send Daytrew in another direction. He'd love nothing more than to rid London of you, and by all that is holy, you've given him another opportunity."

"What do you mean?"

"Your name has already been mentioned; if they can find no one else for this crime, you can be sure it will be delivered to your door," Matthew said. "And now they are digging Slouch up. What if they decide his demise was unnatural? Then there'll be two murders to account for."

"Get out!" Myles' voice shook with temper.

Matthew didn't move.

Myles rounded the table. "I said ...."

"I heard you well enough," Matthew growled.

"GET OUT!" Myles' voice was laced with venom.

Matthew took half a step backwards; changing his mind, he advanced on Myles with lightning speed, his right fist catching tight hold of the cloth of the younger man's nightshirt, and he hauled him close. Surprise rendered Myles immobile in the fierce grip. "I've lost one son, an' I'll fight the Devil before I lose another."

Before Myles could reply or drag himself from Matthew's grip, he was thrown backwards, landing painfully across the top of the chair near the fire. Turning his back on Myles, Matthew carefully refitted his bonnet and reached for the door handle. "I'll be off to find a shovel to dig you out of another pile of shit."

The door closed loudly in its frame before Myles had a chance to extricate himself from the tangle of bed robes he had been left heaped in.

Damn, Matthew to Hell!

Twice!

Myles tried to push himself awkwardly from the chair. The rucked gown had ensnared one leg, and he'd landed on the fabric. Trapped, he was forced to roll indecorously onto the floor. Finally, on all fours, he pulled himself free of the snare of fabric and found himself being regarded by a puzzled Amica.

"Don't you start yowling at me," Myles grumbled at the cat as he pulled himself upright, hauling the gown back around his shoulders.

Reseated at his desk, Myles pushed the papers aside; the allure of the numbers was lost. He drew a glass towards him with a shaking hand and filled it.

"Damn you, Matthew," he said again.

Uttridge had been right, on two counts. Daytrew would be calling to ask questions and that the earthly remains Of Eldridge Slouch were to be dug up, but on the latter point none of them could have guessed what the result of that exercise would be.

The exhumation from St Bride's churchyard of Master Slouch had drawn a crowd. London was a city used to death; the sight of bodies wasn't rare, but the removal of a buried sanctified corpse consigned to the earth in the hope of resurrection was an event. Especially when it belonged to a Londoner as well-known as Slouch. His botchers shop was the largest in the city. Everyone knew where it was; rags were never thrown away or burnt, and even the more well-off of the city's inhabitants would send a servant to Slouch with a sack of rags to exchange for coins. The city's poor would scratch through the gutters and dumps, collecting pieces of cloth, and if you lost washing drying on the line, you could lay a good wager that it would be destined for Slouch's shop, where few questions were ever asked about the source of the offerings. So it was a good crowd that had assembled to watch old Slouch hauled from his slumber.

Daytrew and his men were present, along with a flatbed cart behind them, for the removal of the corpse. Three of St Bride's diggers, her priest, the Justice and Thomas Cleggston, stood close to the graveside.

Thomas Cleggston stood between Daytrew and the Priest, and waved an arm in the direction of the men leaning on their shovels, their instruction to begin. As the earth began to be cleared from the grave, he turned to Justice Daytrew and said, "Hill's men are efficient; I'd wager that the bells will not have struck again by the time they reach the bottom."

Daytrew didn't reply. He just nodded and kept his eyes on the pit.

Cleggston didn't give in. He was a man who dressed like nobility and wrapped himself in a layer of self-importance. His wife was a cousin to the Marquesss of Exeter and had brought him a modest estate near Leicester. He'd unfortunately lost both his wife to the sweating sickness and his lands when he made the decision to back Northumberland's bid to take the throne. When Mary took the crown, his property was forfeited, and his poverty eventually brought him to the White Hart. He'd remained there since, housed in the tavern, his food and ale provided for him, and on occasion, Master Drew, the tailor, delivered clothing befitting his rank. And Cleggston was happy to have retained his noble veneer, and in the White Hart, the only jewel that outshone him was the owner. It's not hard to be noticed when you're the only butterfly on the dunghill, as Myles Devereux had told him, and being vain, Cleggston saw that as something to be cherished.

Myles had recognised his use, and Cleggston leant a degree of respectability to Devereux's dealings with the parish and the church. He was here now in this role. Myles Devereux interred the parish dead, and the diggers were in his pay and under the charge of Cleggston.

The spectators had been banished from the churchyard, but they were sat on or leaning over the walls watching the free entertainment.

The priest, Kemp, was not about to let the proceedings commence without stamping his own authority upon the occasion. He subjected those standing with shovels ready and the silent crowd to a lengthy sermon before the disinterment began. Finally, making the sign of the cross over the fresh grave, he stepped back, nodded to the three men, and a moment later, shovels were lifting the freshly turned earth from the grave.

It hadn't rained since Slouch had been laid to rest, and the earth was easy to remove, still loose and not yet compacted. Some of those assembled to gawp at the spectacle were standing on the walls now to get a better view of the deepening pit. The mound of earth continued to grow; the only noise was from the shovels and the occasional grunt from the diggers as they worked.

The pit was now waist deep, and two of the diggers were inside, the men working rhythmically, avoiding each other's shovel blades and hefting earth to either end of the grave. The third applied his shovel to the fresh earth, moving it to make sure it didn't roll back from where it had come. The men worked on. A man standing on the wall with a child on his shoulders was the first to know what was happening when the child leaned down and whispered in his father's ear.

"They've stopped digging," the words went quickly through the assembled crowd.

The diggers' heads were only visible now above the grave. But the offerings of brown earth being added to the mounds at the ends had stopped. As the crowd watched the priest, Kemp, step forward, rounding the mound of earth, he leaned over and exchanged quiet words with the diggers. A look of concern clouded his face, and he returned to where Daytrew stood with his men.

The priest exchanged a quick word with Daytrew, gesturing with an arm towards the open grave. Daytrew strode past him to stand at the edge of the open pit.

There was a shout of alarm from one of the diggers, and two of Daytrew's men caught the justice by the arms as the side slithered in on top of the diggers.

From the assembled throng of Londoners came a poorly suppressed peel of laughter as the Parish's justice nearly buried himself.

The earth began to appear again at either end of the grave as the diggers removed the collapsed side, and then again the digging stopped. Daytrew, with the priest close at his side, but this time from a safer distance peered into the pit. Daytrew pointed, the digger at the end of the grave shook his head.

There was a hasty exchange between the priest and Daytrew and then digging began again.

The digging stopped an hour later. The gravemen were pulled from the pit and Daytrew and his men left.

The crowd exchanged glances, and a murmur ran along the wall.

The priest, addressing them with his office's full authority, bid them leave, and they did. But they took with them the news of what they had witnessed.

Slouch was missing.

Sam Burnell

Chapter 12

"He's here," Matthew announced.

"He does indeed move slowly. Daytrew is at least half an hour behind the news Cleggston sent. Send him in ...," Myles said, resignedly.

"Very well," Matthew said.

"There's a passing chance his heart will give out on steps on the way up here if we are lucky," Myles said maliciously.

Myles waited in his outer room, seated on the end of the coffer and listened with satisfaction as he heard the heavy, slow, and somewhat uneven tread of Justice Daytrew's feet on the steps outside.

"Justice Daytrew, welcome, like Hermes, hot on the heels of the latest news in London," Myles said sarcastically, as the puffing justice, red cheeked, made his way into the room.

Daytrew's flabby face looked immediately disappointed. "You've heard?"

"News like that travels faster than you do, I am afraid," Myles said smiling. "So, has Kemp, forgotten where he buried poor old Slouch, then?"

"It seems not. The grave had been dug by your men, and the internment was presided over by Kemp," Daytrew said, "And we know the body was there. Your diggers found this,"

Daytrew held forward a piece of linen, muddied, creased and wet.

Myles regarded it with distaste. "Perhaps Slouch thought to take his work with him?"

"Master Devereux, this is no time for levity," Daytrew said, his voice whistling, flapping the filthy scrap of cloth in the air between them.

Myles regarded him with cold eyes, and the justice dropped his gaze to the floor and he swallowed nervously. "So what exactly have you found?"

"It's a piece of the shroud, proof he was interred in the grave," Daytrew pronounced, still waving the ragged remnant towards Myles.

Myles dropped from the coffer top. Made a pretence of being momentarily interested in the cloth and then raised his eyes to meet Daytrew's small, deeply recessed ones. "And?"

Daytrew had reddened even further. "The body has been removed."

"Are you sure you have had the men digging in the right place?" Myles countered.

"Master Cleggston is absolutely positive this is where Master Slouch was laid to rest, and it was a freshly dug grave with no body in it. Why would it have been dug, filled in, and left empty?" Daytrew asked.

Myles shrugged. "Not a question I can answer."

"The men who dug the grave, Master Devereux, are your men, and they are now being questioned closely regarding this matter," Daytrew said, and then continued, "I came here only as a curtesy, to let you know that this has occurred and to allow you to perhaps provide some clarification on the issue."

Myles gawped at the justice. "Clarification?"

"Indeed. Perhaps you are aware of some reason why Master Slouch is not where he should be?"

"And why would you think that I should know where he is?" Myles said.

Daytrew flushed, and shifted his weight from one foot to another, making the gown that hung from his belly sway. Clearly uncomfortable with what he needed to say, he managed, "Master Devereux, it is known ... that last year .... When the weather was particularly bad, and there was a flood in the graveyard at St Bride's ..... that you were forced to store the dead of the parish in the crypt."

Myles glared at him. Daytrew took half a step backwards.

"You have not come here to question me about last year; you have come here to question Master Devereux about something that has occurred far more recently," Matthew intervened quickly.

Daytrew, relieved, turned to Matthew, who he clearly found a lot less intimidating than Devereux. "It was raised that something similar could have occurred and that this would account for the absence of Master Slouch's body."

"The weather has been good, I cannot think that there is any reason at all why poor Master Slouch would not be interred where he should be, and as you did say yourself, Kemp the priest, did say he had seen the body lowered into the ground," Matthew said, then to Devereux. "The issue is a puzzle that I am afraid we do not have the answer to."

Matthew was glaring at him, but Myles had no intention of humouring Daytrew and he flung his arms wide. "Kemp saw the body laid to rest and covered with earth, how should I have any notion as to why he's not there. Perhaps the fingers of the Devil have reached up and claimed him."

Daytrew paled, and his right hand strayed to the cross that hung from his neck. "You cannot be suggesting that is why his body is gone? Surely, it would just be his eternal soul that would be claimed."

Myles stared hard at the justice, and shook his head. "Who knows what happens, Daytrew, once the earth is packed back in the hole and the sods laid over the top?"

"That would be terrible for Master Slouch," Daytrew managed, his mind clearly grappling with the concept of a body being snatched from beneath.

"Perhaps these are questions that should be directed towards Kemp," Myles said, folding his arms.

Daytrew shook his head. "Kemp was as perplexed as Master Cleggston about what the explanation could be."

"Perhaps some closer questioning of the priest may be in order; it is, after all, his cemetery and he did preside over unfortunate Master Slouch's internment; perhaps there was some irregularity during the service that could account for this?" Myles said.

Daytrew's eyebrows raised. "What are you alleging, sir?"

Myles smiled. "Nothing at all, only that your answers probably lie closer to St Bride's than to the White Hart."

"I shall raise these issues with Kemp, as you suggest. The diggers are being questioned as well, but when they opened the grave, they were as baffled as we all were," Daytrew said.

"It could be that there is no earthly reason for what has occurred," Myles said, shaking his head with a look of concern. "Of course, there is another explanation, one so terrible that I would rather not speak of it."

Daytrew's brows rose. His voice hushed, he asked nervously, "What would that be, sir?"

Myles shook his head. "There is no other evidence for it. I should not have said anything."

"What, sir, please, if it would aid my investigation, you must impart your thoughts," Daytrew urged.

"When you put it like that, I suppose I have little choice," Myles said seriously, tugging his chin thoughtfully.

"What is this terrible explanation?" Daytrew asked again.

Myles fixed him with a cold stare and said gravely. "A revenant."

Matthew rolled his eyes.

Daytrew's eyes widened. "You mean …."

Myles nodded slowly, his voice serious, he said. "It does seem to fit with the facts. These are issues for Kemp, don't you think?"

Daytrew, more than happy to bring the meeting to a close, excused himself, Matthew escorted the justice from the Hart and then stomped back up the stairs. Flinging the door open, he fixed Myles with an angry stare. "A revenant? Why did you say that? You know how much of a fool Daytrew is."

Myles smiled. "It fits the facts, does it not?"

"What? That Slouch's rotting corpse is missing because he's arisen from the grave as one of the Devil's own. Come on! More than likely, that fool Cleggston has had them digging in the wrong place; they're not likely to argue with him. If he tells them to dig there, then they will. One patch of turned soil looks very much like the next."

"I agree, that is probably very much the case. But it's much more amusing to send Daytrew from here to hunt ghosts! This could be his undoing if we are lucky," Myles mused.

"His undoing, how?" Matthew asked warily.

"The Sherrif might finally realise the fool has to go," Myles replied, a malicious smile on his face.

"I'd rather deal with Daytrew the fool, and don't forget, we've a hold over him which we might not have over his successor," Matthew warned.

"Sadly true," Myles accepted.

"Anyway, I thought revenants were supposed to return to their earthy graves during the day?" Matthew said.

Myles laughed. "Who knows. Please don't tell me you believe in them?"

Matthew wagged a finger towards Myles. "There's more to heaven and hell than you can fathom. Just remember that."

Myles waved a hand airily. "Yes, of course, now get that fool Cleggston up here so we can find out what actually happened to Slouch."

Cleggston had one good set of clothes, tailored for him by Drew, whose brief had been to produce the desired image for minimal cost. The lack of expense was starting to show. The lace cuffs were now no more than a mat of greyed, tangled and limp threads. Something looked like it had set its teeth to the shirt collar, and the lace, like that on the cuffs, had lost all pretence of delicacy. The plumes from his hat looked as if the bird they had come from had lost a battle; one was snapped in half, a tuft only of the second remained, and the final one hung limply, the quill broken partway along. His hose were moth-eaten, his boots were wrapped with leather cord holding the tops to the soles, and his doublet was bereft of half its buttons. Cleggston, from a distance, looked the part, but the closer you got, the more threadbare the facade. Annoyingly, Myles accepted that he would have to address Master Cleggston's appearance.

"Where did you put Slouch?" Myles got straight to the point.

"He should have been where we dug, the marker was still in place. Master Devereux, I have no idea where he is. Justice Daytrew seems to think I was misleading them, but it's not true, I have no reason to."

"Are you very sure you've not placed him elsewhere?" Myles asked again.

"Quite sure, Master Devereux. I've only had the men dig the one grave in the last ten days, and it was this one, so there is no chance of confusing it with another. All the other burials this week were in the communal grave, this is the only one that was cut for a single internment," Cleggston explained.

"And you are quite sure that he was put into the pit? Did you see him lowered in?" Myles pressed.

Cleggston nodded. "I did. Well, I saw a shrouded body lowered in. But it belonged to someone with a spare frame, which Master Slouch did have. I didn't see the *actual* body, that was sewn inside."

"So there was a body dumped into the pit? Where is it now?" Myles demanded.

Cleggston shrugged. "I wish I knew. Justice Daytrew was most harsh in his questioning, and Hill's men are being most closely questioned as well."

"Do you think someone removed it?" Myles asked.

"Who would want to do such a thing?" Cleggston said.

"No idea. But the fact remains that we have a grave without its body. Could the grave have been reopened and Slouch removed and then it filled in again?" Myles asked.

"Well, I suppose. The earth is freshly turned, so it's a simpler task than digging out a fresh grave from the ground it would be much easier. But it would attract attention, wouldn't it?" Cleggston said, his brow furrowed.

"I doubt it was done during the day," Myles pointed out.

"If it was night, then they'd need a light? Surely? Someone would be bound to have seen them then," Cleggston said.

"Would they?" Myles remembered a full moon illuminating Amica as she sat on the sill, and that had been when he had heard that Slouch was dead. He would have been buried soon after, so there would still have been plenty of light from a waning moon to illuminate the graveyard. "I want to know who dug that grave out, Clegg. Find out."

"I'm not sure, sir, how I would do that? I am sure it wasn't Hill's men," Cleggston sounded confused.

"If someone wants a grave emptying quickly, then you are going to need someone who is used to that work; it'd take anyone else most of the night otherwise. Ask some questions, find out. It is very much in your own interest to do so," Myles finished.

"I don't understand?" Cleggston said.

Myles ran his eyes up and down Cleggston, a look of distaste on his face. "Find out, and I'll summon Master Drew."

"Oh," Cleggston said, and a broad smile split his face. "You can depend on me, Master Devereux, I shall leave no stone," then tapping his nose, he grinned and added, "or clod unturned."

"Yes, quite. To work, Clegg," Myles waved his hand towards the door. Thomas Cleggston was dismissed.

Matthew tugged at his short, neat beard. "You've made a good point there."

"What's that?" Myles said, one eyebrow raised.

"It's back-breaking work, and someone will undoubtedly have been paid well to do it. If you are right, and Slouch was dug up, and this isn't just some idiotic error on Cleggston's part," Matthew said.

"I'd like to think it was. But why would there be a grave dug and filled in empty? Plus, there were witnesses to Slouch being dropped in the hole," Myles replied.

"I'll get the lads to ask about; put the word about in the tap room that we are looking for the man who did this," Matthew nodded, extending an arm in the direction of the drinking room below them.

"It's more than likely there were more than one of them, if you wanted to empty a grave quickly it'd be slow work for one man," Myles said thoughtfully.

Chapter 13

Myles' crossed the room to his bed on bare feet and trod on something prickly and dry.

"What have you dragged in here now, Amica?" Myles grumbled, his eyes on the dried twigs caught in the threads of his carpet. Suddenly, he realised what they were, and flung the cover back on the bed. The small lavender bag had been torn open, the string pulled free, and the dried flowers were spread across the sheets. "You, bastard, cat! Where are you?"

Amica, immediately aware of his displeasure, was perched on the window sill and mewled loudly.

Myles cursed and brushed the lavender to the floor.

Bloody cat.

Meanwhile, in the tap room below, Matthew's eyes roamed over the sparsely-filled tavern. There were few patrons. The hour was late, the kitchens closed, the warming fires in the two hearths had been dampened down to discourage drinkers from being tempted to linger. There came a point every evening when coin was no longer flowing into Devereux's tavern. There were still around two dozen men idling amongst the benches, nursing cups down to the dregs, and yet not ready to leave the tavern. Conversation, the lingering warmth from the dead fires, the company or simply because they had nowhere else better to be, kept them in the tavern for as long as they could remain there.

If there was entertainment, a cock-fight, or the players were visiting the Hart, then the hour would grow late before Matthew turned out the last of the customers. But tonight, there was nothing of note; the weather for summer was annoyingly poor, and the remaining men lingered only to prevent themselves from receiving a soaking.

"Come on, out with you," Matthew announced, striding into the room.

"Master Matthew, I's only just had my cup filled," Carl Hinter complained.

"Hinter, you've been holding onto those dregs for an hour, sling it down your throat and be gone," Matthew said, waving an arm towards the tavern door.

Hinter looked sadly at the warm remains in his cup, shrugged and emptied it into his mouth before rising and following the other men who had lingered towards the tavern door. When they were all out, Matthew dropped the two heavy wooden planks into their iron hooks on either side of the door, and it was solidly sealed.

Devereux's rat boys had already begun to emerge from the edges of the room and were moving towards the hearth and the remaining warmth.

"Rogan, come here," Matthew said, crooking his finger towards the boy.

Rogan, eager to obey, and determined in time to become one of Master Matthew's men, bounded towards him eagerly.

"Have you heard about Slouch?" Matthew asked.

Rogan nodded. "Aye, he's gone from his grave. I were there watching them dig 'im up."

Matthew smiled. "I bet you were, and were you dipping a few pockets at the same time."

"Not me, sir," Rogan said defensively.

"I'd be disappointed if you hadn't, just don't get bloody caught, lad. You'll be no use to me and Master Devereux if you've a hand missing, remember that," Matthew warned.

"Aye, I will," Rogan said, a severe expression on his face.

"I'd like to know who dug up old Slouch, and this," Matthew produced a coin and held it up between them, "is yours if you can find out."

Rogan's eyes were wide and fixed on the silver.

"I think it would be more than one man, they would have worked quickly through the night to do it, and it must have been done soon after old Slouch was buried. It could be that some of Hill's men were involved, I don't know. So you use those ears of yours and find out what you can and let me know," Matthew said, then with this thumb, he flipped the coin into the air and snatched it from Rogan's view.

"I will, sir; you can trust me," Rogan said enthusiastically.

"Good," Matthew straightened and hid a smile as the boy gave a salute before darting off to join his companions near the hearth.

When Daytrew presented himself back at the White Hart, his confidence was bolstered by the man who accompanied him, one Belvadier Richson, lawyer and personal assistant to the coroner. Much to Daytrew's relief and Devereux's annoyance, Richson took the lead.

Richson entered two steps ahead of Daytrew - it was clear he felt he had authority over the justice. His tailoring wasn't as expensive as Devereux's, but it wasn't far away. Around his neck, a thick square link chain led down to an enamelled plaque that declared him to be the coroners man. The buckles in his boots were embellished with polished emeralds. His cloak, pinned back on one shoulder, revealed beneath a rich blue silk lining with gold piping that hatched the fabric into diamonds. Myles found himself momentarily distracted by the tailoring.

"Sir, it is poor news that brings me here," Richson said.

The gold thread gave it the appearance of the panes in a window. Myles rested his eyes on it for a moment longer - he needed Drew to find out who tailored Richson's clothes.

"Sir, it is an issue of a somewhat delicate nature, privacy would be preferred," Richson tried again.

Myles tilted his head – it would be better if a fur trim were used, especially if it the fur was a light colour and matched well with the ...... Matthew's elbow interrupted his thoughts.

"So, you're Daytrew's tongue now are you? Bringing the bad news, he dare not," Myles sneered at Richson.

Any pretence at cordiality dropped from Richson's face. "I've been told that you can be difficult to deal with. But I can advise you that any words you send in my direction will have as little effect as rain on slate. I am not a man whose composure can be unwound."

"Thank you for the warning. You'll forgive me if I try a little harder. Even slate wears given sufficient time," Myles said, his dark eyes fixed on Richson's hazel ones. "What unpleasantness is it wish to impart?"

"This is no matter for levity, sir. A multitude of crimes have been committed," Richson reprimanded.

"This is London, daily fayre for the city," Myles replied. "So which particular indiscretion has brought you to my door?" Myles drawled.

"Wybert Grey, sir," Richson said, a sparkle in his hazel eyes, knowing his words were ones Devereux had not expected. "You are in the habit of conducting business with him?"

Myles eyes regarded Richson with a cold stare. "I thought you were here to discuss a crime?"

Richson smiled. "There are many puzzles and questions to ask, I am afraid. Wybert Grey, are you in the habit of doing business with him?"

Myles folded his arms and fixed Richson with a serious stare. "Has Grey committed a crime, or has one been committed against him?"

Richson ignored Myles and said, "I simply want to know if you are in the habit of doing business with Wybert Grey."

Myles gave a harsh laugh. "The word simply to a lawyer is not the same as it is to a layman like myself."

"It is a straightforward question, a simple yes or no will suffice," Richson said, his voice rising a little.

Myles snapped his fingers and waited while Matthew poured wine and then handed him the glass, he made no attempt to offer Richson or Daytrew any. Myles sipped the wine, set the glass down, and said, "Hardly a habit, Richson. We have players perform occasionally at the White Hart and he prints sheets to advertise the events."

"Anything else?" Richson said.

"He spends his coin in my taverns," Myles said, folding his arms and wondering what dead end Daytrew had led him down.

"I see," was all Richson said, there was a slight air of sadness attached to his words.

"What is this Richson?" Myles said, stepping towards the man. "I'm not keeping any secrets; that worm comes in here and spends more than he probably should on drink and dice, but that is not my responsibility, is it?"

"It's not his attendance at the White Hart that is the issue," Daytrew interrupted.

"Well, then. What is?" Myles said feeling his temper beginning to rise. When it came to Justice Daytrew Myles always was very short on patience.

"Justice Daytrew, if you please. I am capable of asking a few simple questions on my own," Richson said.

Myles grinned. "The lawyer in you is coming out again! More simple questions indeed."

"Master Grey has said that last year, in the autumn, his mother passed away from the sweating sickness," Richson said, pausing for effect.

"My condolences .... So?" Myles said with sarcasm.

"Justice Daytrew has the details," Richarson said.

Daytrew cleared his throat. "He sold her clothes and what linen there was to Master

Eldridge Slouch; few will, as you know, involve themselves in trading with what has belonged to those who have died of the sickness, and Slouch, it seemed, was not averse to that. Although Master Grey did say that he received a pittance in return for what Master Slouch's women took from his mother's home ….."

"Stop rambling, man," Myles interrupted.

Daytrew regarded him with a cold gaze. "Master Grey said that when he had occasion to collect his money from Slouch at his office, you were already there and were involved in a heated argument with Master Slouch."

Myles glared at Daytrew. "What are you trying to allege?"

Richson spoke. "Justice Daytew is alleging nothing, Master Devereux. I am asking only if you remember the occasion and the reason for the argument."

"It is some long time past. Master Devereux visited Slouch on numerous occasions, and I am sure he cannot remember one meeting from another," Matthew said quickly, drawing Richson's attention.

"Can we infer from this that your master was in the habit of arguing with the late Master Slouch when you met him at his workshops?" Richson asked Matthew.

Myle's expression froze. "Thank you, Matthew."

Myles' words drew the eyes of the other two men in the room. "I may, on occasion, have argued with Slouch. After all, that is the nature of business, is it not? What does Grey remember of this particular conversation that I don't?"

"Well, he seemed to think that you were at odds with Master Slouch, accusing him of cheating and paying you less than you were owed," Richson said pointedly.

Myles swallowed his first reply and said instead. "This I cannot recall. Did Grey have anyone with him who may have also recalled this conversation?"

Myles didn't miss the expression of acute disappointment that slackened Daytrew's face, but Richson replied, "Unfortunately, no, but it still raises questions that require answers."

"Does it? Grey recalls overhearing an argument that I cannot recall having. He was not a party to it, but outside, he didn't witness it, and no one else overheard it, I think." Myles paused. "There are no further answers required. Matthew, if you will."

Matthew did not hesitate. Before Richson and Daytrew could complain, the door was open, and Matthew's strong arm gently pressured them towards it. He spoke as he steered the officials from the room: "I am sure if Master Devereux recalls anything else of relevance, he will send a message directly to your office. Good day to you, Master Richson, Justice Daytrew."

Myles watched them leave, his eyes still on the wooden door when it swung back to close in the frame.

Bloody Daytrew.

The door wasn't idle for long. Daytrew and Richson disposed of, and Matthew was soon back in the room.

"You know why this has happened, don't you?" Matthew growled.

"I feel you are about to tell me," Myles said resignedly.

"You humiliated him! Why?" Matthew said, advancing on Myles.

"Stop this! Would you have me molly to every man in the taproom? Lend my ear to every complaint, every whisper of unfairness and every bloody petition? Would you let them solicit me with their tireless needs from morning until night? Well, would you?" Myles demanded.

"That's not what I meant," Matthew said defensively.

"They ...." Myles stabbed a long finger towards the open window. "Can come here on Friday. Then I will listen. I bend to no man's bidding."

Chapter 14

The note was delivered by a boy, well dressed compared to Devereux's rat boys and clearly nervous about having to enter the White Hart. He hopped from foot to foot, his eyes darting around the taproom, too nervous to approach any of Devereux's men, so he waited with the rest of those gathered on Friday to pay their dues or petition for a new loan.

Matthew dropped easily down the stairs. He had seen the lad earlier and was surprised to find him still there. He'd assumed he was accompanying his master, but most of those who'd wanted to see Devereux had now done so, and the tap room was empty. Matthew crooked a finger in his direction, and the boy darted forward, his arm outstretched. He stopped dead, holding toward Matthew a folded note.

Matthew frowned. "What's this, then?"

"For M ... M... Master Dev .... Dev ... Devereux," the boy stammered.

Matthew took it and unfolded the sheet. "Your master is Finney, the apothecary?"

"Y... y.... y....yes master," the boy stammered.

Matthew flapped the paper towards him, and the boy jumped. "And this bill is for

Master Devereux. Did Finney give you any other instructions?"

The boy shook his head.

Matthew leaned down towards the boy. "Now, remember this message, and you be sure to deliver it to your Master. Tell him this bill is an impudence he is about to regret."

The boy paled.

"Repeat what I just told you," Matthew growled.

"I .... I have to tell ...."

"Yes, what do you have to tell your master?" Matthew said.

"Th ... Th ... it's an indupence he will regret," The boy stammered.

"An impudence, you dolt," Matthew corrected.

"Im ...impudence," the boy said weakly.

Matthew wafted the page at him again. "Go on, be gone."

The boy ducked out of Matthew's range and exited the tavern door a moment later.

Matthew cast the note down on the desk before Myles. "A bill from Finney for you."

"Finney?" Myles said, his fingers flattening the sheet.

"The Apothecary," Matthew said grinning.

"Since when did we start using ..... this is Slouch's bill! The arrogant bloody cur," Myles exploded.

Matthew, laughing, said, "I didn't think you'd be very happy about it."

"Did you read this?" Myles said, "He's titled it 'bills pertaining to the botching Shop Ex of Master Slouch.'"

Myles, on his feet, rounded the desk, waving the bill like a flag. "Get my horse. Now! Have you seen the amount that Finney is demanding?"

Matthew took the paper from Myles' hands. "I'll deal with it. I don't want Finney dropping dead in a fit of fear and adding to the current liturgy of complaints against you."

Myle's face darkened.

Matthew ducked beneath the low door into the crowded interior of Finney's shop. A hanging bunch of dried rosemary snared his bonnet and he pulled it from his head, tucking it into his belt. The boy he had seen earlier, now wearing a linen apron, jumped when he recognised Matthew.

Matthew smiled. "Get to. Fetch your master."

Finney arrived a few minutes later, a similar apron over his clothes, the large front pocket sprouting cord, dried thyme and a pair of cutters. He straightened his shoulders, pointed his chin towards the ceiling, and faced Matthew without apparent fear.

"You know why I'm here?" Matthew said, casting the bill down on the counter before the apothecary.

Finney swallowed. "This is only an accounting of items provided to Mistress Delwyn, she indicated that Master Devereux, as the new owner would be paying in future for the essentials needed for that business."

"Essentials!" Matthew blurted, a thick powerful forefinger stabbing the bill. "What, pray tell, is this at a cost of three pounds?"

Finney fished his glasses from the apron pocket, settled them on his nose, and turned the paper towards him. Matthew folded his arms across his chest, knowing full well that Finney knew the exact contents of the bill.

"Well?" Matthew demanded.

"It's naytron, sir, of the finest quality," Finney said, removing his glasses and tucking them back into the apron pocket.

"And naytron is what?" Matthew demanded.

"It's a fine salt mixed with a herbal infusion and rosemary," Finney replied.

"Any what's it used for?" Matthew demanded.

Finney shrugged. "I made it specifically as Mistress Delwyn directed."

"And you've supplied this before?" Matthew asked.

Finney nodded. "Once before, sir."

"Any Slouch paid for this?" Matthew asked.

"He did, Mistress Delwyn settled the account," Finney replied.

"Well," Matthew lifted the sheet from the counter, "you can direct this towards her if you like, but mark this, Finney, this reckoning has nothing to do with Master Devereux."

"But sir, it's expensive and used in his business," Finney said, his voice raising a degree.

"Exactly, and ordered by him and *NOT* by Master Devereux," Matthew said.

The loss of a significant sum was making Finney braver than he usually would be. "Surely you can understand that the debt is attributable to the business, and this is now Master Devereux's concern, so I am told."

"And what is Master Devereux's concern is none of yours. Your debtor is Finney dead and buried, and his debt has died with him," Matthew said.

"Well, that's not quite true, is it?" Finney shot back, his chin jutting forward obstinately.

"What do you mean?" Matthew growled.

"He's not dead, and buried is he? Indeed, is he dead? Was there ever a body, no one seems to know," Finney said, waving a stained finger towards Matthew.

"If that's the case," Matthew said, grasping Finney's apron and hauling him close, "and Slouch is still alive, then the debt rests squarely with him, doesn't it?"

The bill was obviously worth more to Finney than Matthew had anticipated, and the apothecary glowered at Matthew and said, "I'd be very wary of your Master if I were you. The word is that it's his doing that Slouch is missing, and there are reports Slouch has been seen near the botchers this past week—at night!"

"What?" Matthew released the little man.

"You heard. If you don't believe me go, and ask Mistress Delwyn," Finney said stepping away from Matthew.

Matthew didn't want to go to the botchers shop, but after Finney's words regarding the Delwyn woman he knew he had little choice. When he arrived he'd expected to see more of Devereux's men and not just Cutlake.

The sound of the women singing met Matthew as he opened the door, the workshop was full, and Cutlake was idling against a wall near the open door to the yard at the back. Matthew jerked a thumb at him and Cutlake pushed himself away from the wall and joined Matthew in the small corridor outside the workshop. Matthew, closed the door, not wanting an audience for this conversation.

"Where's the rest of them?" Matthew asked.

"It seemed a waste, Master Matthew. Daytrew's men are no longer here, and it's one thing having them here during the day, but there's no need in the evening, so I send the lads back to the Hart," Cutlake said, then smiling added. "Once the place is locked up, there's not much for them to do, is there?"

"True, if Daytrew's men have left there's no real need for them at all. What's brought me here though is an accusation from Finney that Slouch has been seen. This can't be true?" Matthew said.

Cutlake laughed. "I doubt that very much?"

"Well then, why are the tongues of London clacking like geese with the gossip then?" Matthew said.

"One of Peggy's women, Daisy, swore he'd been back at the botchers shop. She was fairly petrified and you know what women are like, fire can't spread as fast as the foolish tales they tell," Cutlake said, shaking his head.

"Were they foolish? His body is missing, and I'm beginning to wonder if he was even buried in the first place, Cutlake. That would be an explanation for all of this, wouldn't it?" Matthew replied, his thumbs had found his belt.

Cutlake frowned. "I suppose, but sir, Daisy isn't one you can rely on; the woman had a fright in the night and blamed it on Slouch."

"Are you sure?" Matthew pressed.

Cutlake's face was serious. "Very. The woman's deaf and dumb."

"How has she told them it's Slouch?" Matthew exclaimed, "This becomes more ridiculous by the very moment."

Cutlake nodded in agreement.

"You warn those damned women that if there is any more of this gossip seeping from their workroom that they'll be out on their arses," Matthew said, then suddenly changing his mind. "Are they all in there now?"

Cutlake nodded.

"I'll do it myself!"

Matthew opened the door to the botchers shop and the smell, lye, urine with an undercurrent of rot met his nose. None of the women were outside in the yard working; all were gathered around the central work table, and Peggy was handing out small bread loaves from a basket. Some of the women wrapped them in cloth to take back to their families, some sank their teeth into them eagerly. Peggy stopped when she saw him, a loaf held towards one of the women who retracted her hand when she saw Matthew.

"Master Matthew, sir," Peggy said smiling and gifting him the sight of her ruined teeth.

Matthew ran cold eyes over the women. "I've enough trouble in my life without having to deal with your scaggling wenches. It seems tongues have been wagging, and unhelpfully so, as well."

"Ah," Peggy said, her smile thankfully disappearing.

"So you know what I am referring to? I'll have no more tales of revenant's, the dead rising and other child's tales seeping from here. Is that understood?" Matthew's loud voice boomed. "Daisy? Where is she?"

"The lass has gone, sir," Peggy said.

"Gone?" Matthew questioned.

"Aye. I'd 'ave turned her off anyways, but the silly creature took herself back to the tavern. We've not seen her since, 'ave we?" Peggy said, surrounded by the shake of heads from the other women.

Matthew glared at them, each of them careful to avoid his gaze. Banging his fist down on the table. "One more word from here that makes it to the streets outside and you'll all be turned out, do you damned well understand?"

There was no reply. The women stood motionless, their eyes fixed on the floor.

"For God's sake, feckling bloody creatures, it's like trying to talk to sheep. Do you understand me?" Matthew banged the table again, the two women nearest to him started, but he received no reply.

"Master Matthew, as you say they have the ken of sheep, but I will make sure they understand," Peggy said quickly.

Matthew stabbed a thick forefinger through the air towards her. "You had better. If I come back here again it will be to throw you all in the gutter."

Myles held up a hand to stop Matthew from speaking, what he was saying made no sense. "Slouch was where?"

"Probably nowhere, but one of those foolish women had said she'd seen him back at his botchers shop standing near the doorway, and the rest of them have spread that news like fire across a heath. It'll be the gossip of London by now!" Matthew said furiously.

"And you think this is my fault?" Myles rounded the desk.

"I do! And Wilbert Grey, and Wignot!" Matthew continued.

"Speak your mind, Matthew," Myles growled at him.

"Aye, I will, damn you. You'll burn if you are not careful, and you'll drag everyone around you into the pit at the same time. You …." Matthew leaned close to Myles and said slowly. "Are not safe to be let out."

"Get out," Myles took a step towards the other man.

Matthew grinned. "As you say."

A moment later Matthew had slammed the door behind him and Myles, reading what he meant to do, failed to reach the door before he heard the key rattle in the lock on the other side. Five inches of church oak were now between him and the outer room. Myles beat his fists against the closed door, he doubted even that the sound could be heard on the other side.

Chapter 15

Myles paced the room cursing, his breath coming in short gasps. It took some time before his temper was his under control. Banging his fist down on the table, he made the ink pot rattle in its holder, his eyes came to rest on Slouch's book. Sitting at his desk slowly, he began to leaf through the pages; some were still dog-eared where he had found the name, Harrington.

What was the connection? Indeed, was there one? Myles rubbed his eyes and pushed the book from him; rising, he turned and gazed out of the window. The yard was quiet. Night had descended on London. A movement near the gate caught Myles' eye. He wasn't the only one who noticed it. The two men Matthew had guarding the yard descended on the dark corner, and a moment later, a complaining boy, Myles, recognised as one of the Hart's rat boys was being shoved towards the back of the tavern by the men. "Go on, yer little shit, off with you."

A moment later, the yard was still again. The rat boy had scurried inside, and the men had returned to their watch under a lean-to out of the wind. The bells at St Bride's rang out, and Myles dropped his hands from the sill and retreated back into his room, which was now his prison.

At first, he thought it was Amica, the sound of scrattling on the wood ledge outside his always-open window. Turning towards it, and about to admonish his cat, he saw instead a leather cap, the ear flaps dangling and a face with an uncut fringe obscuring the eyes staring at him.

Rogan.

"Sir, I need to tell you something," Rogan said urgently, looking back quickly over his shoulder to see if his ascent had been observed.

Myles rounded the desk. "In quick, come on."

The boy didn't hesitate. A second later, his rag-wrapped feet were over the sill, and he landed lightly, crouching down so his head could not be seen from the window.

Myles folded his arms and regarded the child. "Well?"

"Master Matthew asked me to find out something, an' I did. He said I'd to come straight back an' tell him what I found out, an' that it was important, but he's not 'ere. So's I came to see you, Master Devereux," Rogan said boldly.

"And it is right you did," Myles replied, "So, what did you find out?"

"Hill, the gravedigger who works for you, sir, he's working for someone else besides," Rogan announced.

Myles unfolded his arms. "Go on. Tell all."

Rogan, assured by the tone of Myles' voice, continued. "Hill usually spends his coin 'ere, at the Hart. But this last week 'es bin down at the Red Lion, along wi' his lads."

"Although it's annoying he's not spending his coin here, why is this so damning?" Myles questioned.

"Well, sir, I've been down there these last few days watchin' and listening like, an' he got into a fight with Tiny Wattley, one of the diggers who works for 'im. They had a right brawl, and the landlord and his lads hurled them out in the street, but that didn't stop them and they continued. Hill were on top o' Tiny and beltin' 'im around the head, and he's tellin' him again and again that he'll get more than a beatin' if he breathes a word of what they've been doing," Rogan said, and paused.

"Alright, so Hill's been up to no good, do you know what he's done?" Myles asked.

Rogan grinned. "I do. Tiny was one of the rat boys before he worked for Hill, an' we know each other well. When Hill had finished giving him a good hiding I 'elped him up and brought 'im back to the Hart. Master Matthew promised me silver, an' and I told Tiny as much, and said if he'd tell me what Hill had done then I'd let Master Matthew know he's 'elped. But I canna find Master Matthew, an'

Tiny is scared for his life an' hiding in the next yard, an' that's why I came here."

"And what has he done?" Myles demanded.

"He helped Hill dig up old Slouch," Rogan announced, "An' if you'll stop Hill from givin' 'im another beating he'll tell you as much."

Myles cursed. "Why did he dig the old bastard up?"

Rogan shrugged. "Tiny didn't know, all he knows is that Hill forced him to 'elp and Tiny is afeard now of Hill and the Lord for what he's done."

Myles turned towards the door, took one step, and then stopped himself. Matthew wasn't here, and did he really want to share this with him? Perhaps not just yet. There was a purse on the desk. He pulled the strings and fished out a worn silver groat. "Take that, find Tiny, and get yourself to the Angel. Ask for Nathan, and tell him I've sent you there for safekeeping. Give him that. Do you understand?"

Rogan nodded.

"Who do you ask for?"

"Nathan, and tell 'im Master Devereux has sent me to the Angel for safekeeping," Rogan said gravely.

"And there'll be two of these for you in good time," Myles said, depositing the coin in the boy's filthy hand. "Now, be off with you."

Rogan stepped towards the door, and Myles caught his arm. Shaking his head, he pointed towards the window. "It's best if no one else sees you."

Rogan grinned and, turning, jumped onto the sill with an agility that matched Amica's. Myles watched the boy silently and competently traverse the roof to the left and then drop down into the yard before disappearing into the shadows.

So Hill had dug up Slouch. Why?

Myles dropped down into his chair and ran his hands through his hair. It had to be linked to the woman they'd found in the bed, the one Uttridge had said was empty, scraped clean from within. He picked up the pen and dipped it in the ink, on a piece of paper he had been using for making notes before completing his ledgers he was about to write down the names Hill and Slouch, when he suddenly stopped. A moment later he wrote down instead naytron.

Myles shuddered.

It wasn't just Amica and Rogan who could make their way quietly from the sill in his room to the yard. He'd done it before. Myles couldn't use the route Rogan had taken, he was three times the weight of the boy and the thin ledge that ran beneath the window wouldn't take his weight. To get down, first, he needed to go up. Wearing what he hoped was his most anonymous cloak, and dressed in dark clothing with the sword from the end of his bed on his back he left the room.

Standing on the sill and using the ledges provided by the dark timber beams of the Hart, he climbed up to her roof. It was a short distance, and the roof on this side was shallow and edged with a stone runnel to direct the water to the yard. Solid footing for the escapee. If anyone in the yard had looked up at this moment, they would have been able to see Devereux clearly as he walked quickly along the roof edge to the corner of the building. Dropping to his knees, he lowered himself down the wall and made an easy descent into the stables of the White Hart.

"Master Devereux?" Davey Langton said, taking a rapid step back, his boot heel caught on a cobble.

Myles rolled his eyes. "Listen to me, Langton. Questions will be asked later, and if you want to keep your one remaining eye it would be wise for you to tell anyone who asks that you've not seen me."

Confusion, at home, roamed over Langton's face. "But sir ..."

Myles grabbed a fistful of Davey's jerkin and pulled himself close. "I do not wish to have been observed. If anyone asks, you tell them you've not seen me."

Understanding had yet to crystalise. "But what if Master Matthew asks?"

"Especially, if Master Matthew asks. You, Langton, are at the bottom of a very tall tree, Matthew is somewhere half-way up and I am at the top. Don't forget that, and your other eye will remain where it is," Myles threatened.

Myles' words had only served to confuse Davey Langton even further. "You want me to go to a tree, sir?"

Myles shook the man in frustration, cursing himself. "If anyone asks if you have seen me today, your answer will be in the negative."

"In the what …."

"For God's sake, Langton, if anyone, particularly Master Matthew, asks, you've not seen me, is that clear?"

Confusion was now mixing with an inner conflict to do the right thing, and unfortunately, Davey had no idea what that was. "Is that just for today, or forever that I've not seen you?"

"If the parish needs another idiot, I'll tell them you are available. Are you a fool, Langton? It is a simple enough instruction?" Myles said, suddenly, releasing the man; as he did, his eyes rested for a moment on a wide-bladed knife housed in Langton's belt, and another idea occurred to him. "Actually, Langton, I want you to come with me. I'm going to cross London, and I'd rather not do that on my own."

"Aye, Master Devereux," Langton said, accepting a task he understood. "I'll come with you."

A few minutes later, they had both slipped from the back of the White Hart into the city's dark streets. Myles was pretty sure he had not been seen, and taking Langton with him provided him with a degree of protection and ensured the man would not disclose his departure from the tavern.

Matthew unlocked the door, pushed it open with his foot, picked up the tray of food from the top of the coffer, and carried it into Devereux's room. It wouldn't be good if anyone else knew their Master had been locked in his room by his lieutenant.

"Here. I'll not have you starve. I've even brought something for your cat," Matthew said, a conciliatory tone in his voice.

He didn't get an answer.

Devereux was not seated behind his desk, lounging near the fire, or reclining on the ridiculous four-poster bed. The only eyes that met his were those of the cat from where she sat on the sill, regarding him while running her rough tongue along the back of one of her paws.

Matthew slammed the tray down on the table, the cat made a rapid exit from the sill, disappearing from sight, and Matthew, leaning from the window, stared in vain at the empty yard of the White Hart. How had that bloody fool climbed from there without being seen? To raise the alarm that Devereux was missing wasn't a good idea; his absence from the White Hart would not be good for business.

Matthew had expected his return within a few hours. When he wasn't back by the following morning, he made discrete conversational enquiries, but none of the men had seen Devereux. When a whole day had elapsed, and he had not reappeared or sent word back to the tavern, Matthew knew something was very wrong.

His feeling of dread worsened when one of his men bounded up the stairs to report that Justice Daytrew, accompanied by Master Richson and a dozen men at arms were outside the Hart and demanding to speak to Master Devereux.

Settling his bonnet on his head at a satisfactory angle, Matthew said to no one in particular as he walked across the taproom. "Someone find me the Devil's shovel, any I have will not be big enough to shift today's shit."

"I have a warrant for your master's arrest, kindly tell him to produce himself," Richson said.

"I wish I could help, but he's not here," Matthew said, failing to keep a satisfied tone from his words.

"Well, where is he then?" Richson demanded.

Matthew shrugged and said truthfully. "I can't say that I know."

Richson turned to Daytrew. "Have your men search this place and drag him out if you have to."

Matthew waved an arm in a gesture of invitation towards the door of the Hart. "I'll not stop you from looking."

They did look. As Matthew had assured them, there was no trace of Myles Devereux. Richson, not about to leave empty-handed, arrested Matthew to answer for his Master's crimes instead.

Uttridge was longer in arriving than he should have been. When he did, even Matthew was mildly impressed with the lawyer for once. It seemed he kept his nerves for when he was in Devereux's presence. Before the sheriff he was competent and his eyes were bright with the prospect of crossing legal swords with Richson it seemed. The sheriff, the coroner's assistant, Richson, and Daytrew were all in the sheriff's outer office, seated at the table; an elderly scribe was trying his best to note down what was said, although the furious pace of the conversation was against him.

The room was plainly furnished; any opulence was behind the door leading to the sheriff's private rooms. The walls were lined with panelling that had come from elsewhere, and the linenfold lines, carved into the woodwork, on occasion failed to line up. The floor was bare boards, worn deeply near the doorway; there was a fireplace against one wall, but it was never known to be lit. So frequently was the door to the courtyard opened and closed that a fire during the winter months would have been a waste of fuel and good money.

"A thatch is made of many reeds, not just one, Uttridge, and the evidence against Devereux is weighty," the Sherrif pronounced, eyeing Matthew as if he were the culprit.

Uttridge nodded gravely. "There have been serious crimes committed, I agree. I would appreciate it if you would be so kind as to provide me with your case against Master Devereux."

Richson frowned. "You know the facts well enough."

"I am sorry, Master Richson, I don't," Uttridge said.

"For the Lord's sake man. Devereux is known to have wanted to be rid of Slouch to take his business from him, he tried to stop Kemp from entering the house where the woman's body was found with some ridiculous argument relating to access rights, and then when they did get inside he tried to blame the stench on the stream running beneath the house or some dead animal! He's threatened Kemp, had the man in fear for his life, and we now know he forced the priest to allow him to use the crypt to store the deceased of the parish last year. And he's a questionable heavy guard on a wash-house, why would that be one needs to ask? On top of this, he's recently acquired a tannery, and the owner was found swinging from his own beam," the Sherrif blustered.

"An unfortunate and indeed harrowing set of circumstances, but none that can be attributed to the man you have here, surely?" Uttridge turned to Matthew. "The servant cannot be held accountable for the acts of the master, if indeed what you allege are his acts."

The Sherrif banged a fist on his desk. "Richson?"

"The servant can be liable for only his own actions, and the Master can be liable for the acts of his servants. But in this case, there has been no allegation at all that this man has acted in any way that has affected the matters you have outlined. Master Matthew Thwaite had nothing to do with the discovery of the body at Slouch's. Indeed, he wasn't even present, and he has not made any threats to Kemp that I am aware of. There was an alleged argument between Devereux and Slouch, I hear, one overheard through a closed door by Wilbert Grey, but Master Matthew wasn't present inside with his Master or even outside overhearing the argument. If he had been there would at least have been one witness to the incident which at the moment is based solely on the word of Master Grey. And as for the tanner, I agree it was Master Thwaite who found the unfortunate man hanged, and it was he who sent word to the justice of his discovery. But, sir, there has been no allegation that Master Thwaite was involved in any of these allegations you are bringing against his Master. Indeed he has been most helpful, as far as I am aware, no doors were locked against Master Daytrew's men during their search were they?" Uttridge turned his attention to Daytrew.

"No, that is correct. Indeed, Master Matthew did lead us through the Hart and make sure all the doors were open for us," Daytrew accepted.

Richson scowled at Daytrew. "That does not mean he didn't aid his master in his escape or is assisting him in hiding in a place Daytrew's men have yet to look. And why, may I ask, did he place a heavy guard on the botchers? What washhouse requires the that ten armed men watch over it?" Richson scoffed.

"They were there only a few days. None remain now," Matthew said, he'd recalled then when it he had found Devereux missing.

"Yes, I agree, but why?" Richson pressed.

Matthew could hardly say that they had been sent simply because Devereux had no intention of being outnumbered by Daytrew's men. How to say so though without implication wasn't easy. "Master Devereux's orders, I cannot comment on why he made them." It was a poor response, and Matthew knew it.

Richson turned to the sheriff and scoffed. "There is more to this than protecting rotting rags and wenches."

Uttridge took half a step forwards. "It may be the case, but as Master Thwaite has said they were sent there under the orders of his master, and without placing the question before Master Devereux we cannot know the answer. It is contrary to the common law to engage too much in conjecture, as I am sure Master Richson will agree."

Richson scowled at Uttridge as he stopped another conversational route that would damn Myles Devereux even further.

"Allegations only, sadly," Uttridge said, then to Matthew. "Have you been able to answer the sheriff's questions?"

"I have," Matthew said solidly.

"Good. If they have more, are you willing to answer as best you can?" Uttridge asked Matthew.

"Of course," Matthew accepted.

Uttridge turned to the sheriff. "If you have any more questions, please ask."

The sheriff, knowing he had no cause to hold Matthew, waved towards the door. "Out with you," then a ringed finger pointing towards Matthew he said, "I hear Uttridge's words regarding the culpability of the servant, but we both know that you are united in the guilt of your Master. If we find you've been hiding him, and we will, then you can be assured there will be no leniency based on common law."

"I would expect none, sir," Matthew replied.

"And let's not forget there are other matters, matters above the common law, which are under investigation," the sheriff said.

Uttridge's brow furrowed. "Sir, what matters would they be?"

"His master," the sheriff continued to point towards Matthew. "Let us not forget, seats himself in his tavern in a so-called Devil's chair, and he has predicted a revenant, did he not, Master Daytrew?"

Daytrew, pale now, nodded. "Although, he wasn't seated in that chair when he said he suspected a revenant may be the cause of the missing body."

The sheriff rolled his eyes. "But there is one, it is his favoured throne in his tavern, so I hear. And we do not seem to have a revenant, there have been several sightings now of Master Slouch, and we have to wonder if they are not true given that his body is missing," the sheriff said.

This was dangerous ground indeed, and Uttridge dealt with it quickly. "As you say, sir, a matter under investigation. When enquiries are complete, I am sure Master Thwaite will be willing to answer any more questions you have. Well, that seems to draw the meeting to a close, shall we?" Uttridge, his self-assurance gathered around him like a cloak, and his legal file clamped firmly beneath his arm, turned towards the door.

Once they were some way distant from the sheriff's office, Uttridge asked. "You don't know where Master Devereux is, do you?"

"I don't, but I wish I did," Matthew replied, in his mind he could see the chair that sat to one side of the Hart's taproom, used only by Devereux. Before the day was done it would be axed and burnt.

Myles, pleased with himself, opened the door and let himself in to Galveston's office. His bookkeeper was long dead, but the experience had taught Myles an important lesson, if he needed to disappear again, then he'd not have to take to the streets. He'd taken on Galveston's office and the room above; even Matthew didn't know about it. It had been his intention to refurnish it and make it a more suitable place should he need to use it. But when the danger had been removed, so had the urgency, and Galveston's accommodation and office were much as he had left it, complete with the faded bloodstain on the wood floor.

The gaps around the shutters let in enough light for him to see the state the room had been left in. Papers, an ink pot, and several pens still littered the desk. The place was untidy. Daytrew's men had searched it, and the evidence of that was still there to be seen. The ashes raked from the last fire and spread on the hearth, a wood basket upended, draws in the desk open, papers unsorted and scattered, and a chair on its side.

Myles righted the chair and cracked open the shutters, enough to let a little more light into the room but not enough to allow him to be seen inside. Langston, he had dismissed to Galveston's room above. He didn't want anyone to see the man loitering in the street; with his patched eye, he was a target for any passing attention.

Seating himself at the desk, he swept the detritus of Galveston's life to the floor. Inspecting the ink pot, he found it dry and scowled. Annoyingly, he remembered using the contents to disguise the blood stain on the floor. A quick examination of the open draws didn't turn up another either.

He'd have to order his thoughts in his head instead. Myles cast his eyes around the room. The hour was now late, he'd stop here tonight. Matthew would never even consider looking for him here. Leaving the room and stomping up the stairs to where Langston was, he fished in his purse.

"Be quick, pies and wine. And not a word to anyone, do you understand?" Myles said handing Langston a groat.

"Yes, Master Devereux," Langston confirmed, taking the coin he rose to leave.

Myles ran his eyes around the remains of Galveston's bed chamber. It had also been turned over by Daytrew's men. Langston had righted a low pallet bed and had been lounging on it; apart from that, there was little in the room. Several shelves that had contained folded linen which now lay heaped in the dust on the floor, an earthenware slop pot that had been knocked over and cracked, it was clear Galveston had kept his possessions, such as they were, in the office below his bed chamber. Galveston's nightcap still hung from a peg, and next to it was a thick bed robe. Myles helped himself to the bed robe and descended back down the stairs. He considered lighting the fire; there was a tinderbox, and the contents of the log basket, which was strewn on the floor, were enough to make a decent fire. But Myles quickly changed his mind. he smoke might have raised questions about who was in Galveston's old rooms. And questions he could do without right now.

The bookkeeper's bed robe pulled around his shoulders, and with a poor supper provided by Langston on the desk before him, he pondered what to do next.

Chapter 16

Richard Fitzwarren arrived at the White Hart in the early evening. Matthew wordlessly escorted him up the stairs and let him into the outer room.

"He's not here," Matthew said as soon as the door had closed. "Have you seen him?"

Fitzwarren's brow furrowed. "If I knew of his whereabouts, I would not have called to see him, would I?"

"I thought you might have heard something or had word?" Matthew said, exasperated.

"Oh dear, have you misplaced him?" Fitzwarren said, his voice amused.

"No, I haven't. He's not here, and I don't know where he's gone. He's sent no word, and he knows how dangerous it would be if it were known he was absent. It's Friday tomorrow," Mattew said.

Richard laughed. "Of course. Friday when the pilgrims arrive with their offerings to lay them at the feet of their Lord."

"This isn't an amusing matter," Matthew barked.

"I didn't say it was. Did Devereux go voluntarily, or was he forced to leave?" Richard asked.

"I don't know," Matthew said.

"You must know something? You have a guard on all the doors; if anyone took him from here, surely it would have been noticed? Or have standards fallen that badly?" Richard said.

"He wasn't taken. I'd locked him in his room; there were boot marks on the sill, just one set," Matthew was forced to confess.

Richard's eyebrows raised. "Locked in. Well, well, there's a turn of events. Perhaps he doesn't want to return?"

"It wasn't that bad an argument," Matthew said roughly.

"So he's gone. How long?" Richard asked.

"Two days," Matthew admitted. "The last time I saw him he was sat as his desk."

"Can I see the room? I assume you'd like my help?" Richard said, already walking towards the door.

Matthew stepped between Fitzwarren and the door to Myles' room.

Fitzwarren didn't move, but folded his arms across his chest and regarded Matthew with a steady gaze. "Matthew, you know me very well, I'm not likely to steal your Master's secrets, am I?"

"He wouldn't want you in there looking through things you've no business to," Matthew said, rising to his full height.

Fitzwarren sighed. "I am sure he'd turn puce if he knew, I agree. However, the issue at the moment isn't his fury that his privacy has been violated, it is more that he is missing. Do you want to find him?"

Matthew raised a hand to his head and pulled the leather bonnet from it. "You're right. Go, it's not locked."

"Thank you."

Richard seated himself at Myles' desk, his hands hovered over the surface as his eyes took in the items surrounding him.

"What are you looking for?"

"I don't know until I find it," Richard said.

Matthew leaned over Richard, planting his hands on the desk. "We'll not find him here, and I do need to find him?"

Richard looked up, his dark brown eyes repelling Matthew's. "I agree, but where do we look?"

Matthew flung his arms in the air. "I don't know."

"Exactly. The last time you saw him, he was seated here. So let us presuppose there is a connection between something on here and where he is now."

"You can't be certain? He might have taken whatever it was with him?"

"You're right I can't be certain. And Matthew?"

"Yes?"

"Shut up."

"All I said ...." Matthew was silenced when Richard leaned towards him and planted a finger across his lips.

"That's better. So what were you looking at before you left, I wonder?" Richard's hands began to examine the desk and the items on top of it. "No need for you to put anything out of sight, not with the guard you have on the room. So what was it that sent you from here?"

Matthew slapped the bonnet against his thigh. "How long is this going to take?"

Richard ignored him. His elbows on the desk, hands folded and chin resting on top of them, his eyes carefully examined the desk. The top of the ink pot sat next to it. To his right was a pen, laid on the top of the desk. Richard licked his finger and applied it to a mark on the desk near the nib. There was a sheet of paper, one that had been torn from a ledger. It served as a blotting page for Devereux's pen and included various notes in his hand. Beneath it was another sheet with a list of symbols neatly inscribed.

"He made those notes when he was playing with that astrologica, trying to fathom it," Matthew said.

Richard discarded the sheet of meaningless symbols to the desk and picked up Slouch's ledger. It was the same pen that had underlined certain words on the page. Naytron. Myles had underlined this twice. The second line had been made more forcefully, the writer pressuring the nib so much that the end had bent apart, breaking the final part of the line into two. It had clearly meant something to Devereux.

Naytron

3 Pounds

The word was underlined twice.

Richard took the pen, dipped it into the open pot and added another line beneath it. Very likely from the same pen.

"Naytron?" Richard raised his eyes and met Matthew's. "It was the last word written on this sheet with this pen."

"How do you know it was the last word?" Matthew said, straining his neck to get a better look at the page.

"The two lines beneath it cut over some of the other words on this page. Naytron was added last, and Devereux underlined it twice. It was important. I would guess after he wrote it that he discarded the pen here," Richard pointed, "the ink from the nib marked the desk. He was in a hurry, he didn't put the pen away and omitted to return the lid to the ink pot. Why?"

Matthew tapped his finger on the word. "Naytron, it's what was on the bill from the Apothecary, Finney."

"Finney?"

"There, that's Slouch's account book, he used to buy from Finney, when Slouch died Finney tried to send Slouch's bills to Devereux, arguing that as he had control over the business, he should be responsible for its bills, even if they did arise before he bought it," Matthew said.

Richard opened the book and began to leaf through the pages; there were marks next to each entry.

"He told me Slouch didn't use a standard system, so he told me he had marked each of the entries as buyer or seller," Matthew said helpfully.

Richard nodded, still flicking through the pages. Several had the corners turned back, but quick comparison didn't show why. Richard stopped at the last page. The name Finney appeared, and it had again been underlined – recently.

"I'd wager this has something to do with your wayward apothecary. Devereux knew something, and he went to confirm it; that would be my guess," Richard replied, closing the book.

"I've been to see him. Apart from feeling aggrieved that the bill wasn't settled I don't think he would be the reason Devereux is missing," Matthew said. "If there were something else then surely he wouldn't be fighting to get a bill paid."

"How much was it for?" Richard asked.

"Three pounds," Matthew said. "A lot to Finney, no doubt, but not to Devereux."

"Then there is the puzzle of why he left the White Hart without his men, Matthew, why would that be? What is it you are not telling me?" Richard asked. "Slouch's business, a botchers shop, you said; how did Myles take this on? Taverns, gaming and swaphouses are more to his liking?"

"Slouch died, Myles thought his business would be a good addition. I didn't. And I was right," Matthew said.

"Why were you right?"

Matthew flung his arms forward. "Look before you. He's gone, and as you said yourself, it's probably got something to do with the apothecary that was linked to Slouch. I warned the fool, but did he listen?"

Richard rose and held a hand up. "Conjecture, recriminations, and an allocation of blame, which I am sure has been aptly earned, is not going to find him. Start at the beginning, please. Slouch died – then what?"

Matthew turned his back and strode forcefully across the room, plainly in no mood for this conversation. "He was found dead in his bed and buried. He owed us 6 shillings, and Devereux was furious about it. We were riding past his house when he has the damned fool idea of buying the botchers shop. I didn't agree."

"Why's that?" Richard interrupted.

"It's a bloody washhouse full of wenches, not a good business to be associated with," Matthew said.

Richard grinned. "Ah the man liketh to wear clean attire but cares not to know how it got that way. What happened next?"

Matthew shot an angry look in his direction. "Slouch has a house, there was some argument that it had been left to the church, not something Devereux was happy about as he wanted it. There was a meeting at Slouch's house that had been locked up since the old man had been carted from it and a body was found."

"A body?"

"Aye, it seems Slouch's servant girl had been murdered as well and her body hidden inside his mattress stuffing. Clearly murder, but the corpse was rotten and there was little to identify how she had been killed," Matthew said.

Richard's eyebrows raised. "Delightful. What next?"

"The coroner decided to dig up old man Slouch, to see if there were any murder marks upon him, but his body was missing from St Bride's graveyard," Matthew replied.

"Inconvenient. Don't Devereux's men dig the graves?" Richard asked.

"They do. And that's why he got the blame for the missing corpse, and he'd been heard arguing with Slouch over a deal so the implication was he'd killed him to take his business," Matthew said.

"Oh dear. And I can tell by your expression that there's more," Richard said.

"There is. He'd bribed the priest, given him coin to store the dead in the crypt at St Bride's and under questioning with the sherrif he confessed, saying it was forced upon him as he feared for his very life if he did not do as Devereux commanded. Then there was an incident in the tavern, here. There's a man Devereux has no liking for and he stripped him of his livelihood at the card table and the fool hung himself,"

Richard folded his arms. "And knowing Devereux, there would have been plenty of witnesses to him ruining the man's life."

"Just a tavern full!" Matthew said, angrily. "And to lay a golden bloody crown on the top of all of that he told the justice that they needed to be searching for a revenant."

"Anything else?"

"Is that not enough! A tanner is found hanging so Devereux, can have his business, another is dead, his body, interred by Devereux's men, is now missing and a woman's corpse is found mutilated and Slouch is walking the streets at night!"

Richard held his hand up. "What do you mean 'Slouch is walking the streets at night'?"

"Exactly that! One of those bloody women in his botchers shop saw him, the taverns of London are alive with that gossip, I'm surprised you've not heard. So Devereux predicts a revenant, and a few days later, London has one," Matthew said, his temper close to exploding.

"Now that is inconvenient. By walking the streets, what exactly did this woman see?" Richard asked.

"The woman who saw him is a dolt; she's deaf and dumb," Matthew said, "but the other foolish women have taken her tale and spread it."

"Deaf and dumb?" Richard turned to Matthew.

"One of the woman at the botchers shop. How can a dumb idiot woman tell them who she saw? She needs to be bloody careful otherwise it'll be an allegation of the sight and they'll be warming her heels for her," Matthew grumbled.

"What did she look like?" Richard said slowly.

Matthew shrugged. "No idea, she'd gone by the time I went back to warn them I'd cut their clacking tongues out if this happened again."

"Where did she go? Do you know?" Richard asked.

"The Delwyn woman said she'd gone back to the tavern, that's all I know. Good bloody riddance, it's trouble like that we could do without," Matthew said.

"Which tavern? Did she say?" Richard asked.

Matthew nodded his head. "That rat house, the Panyer."

With Langston at his side Myles arrived at the botchers shop. He had expected to see at least two of his men outside, but none were there. Myles' brow creased! Lazy idling bastards! What was the point in placing a guard if it couldn't be seen!

"You, wait here. And remember what I told you?" Myles commanded.

Leaving Langston on the opposite side of the street, he entered the door to the botchers shop.

As he let the door close behind him, Myles realised how quiet the interior was. The sound of the woman singing as they worked was absent, and the sloshing from the channels at the back of the shop where the rags were pounded in the lye was gone. The back doors leading to the yard and the river were closed, and the workshop was in darkness. None of his men were present, nor Daytrew's – it was simply empty.

"Cutlake?"

Myles stepped inside. A moment later, light flooded into the workshop as one of the doors was pulled noisily open; it was Cutlake.

Relief flooded through Myles. "Cutlake! Where are the men?"

"Master Matthew sent word for them to return to the Hart," Cutlake said, sounding a little confused.

"And Daytrew's men?" Myles asked.

"Oh, they've been gone a few days, as soon as the inquest was held into that poor girls demise," Cutlake replied.

"And the women?" Myles continued.

"Peggy's got them all further down the brook washing rags," Cutlake said.

"And she's with them?" Myles said quickly.

Cutlake nodded, concern on his face. "What's wrong, sir? Should I not have let them go?"

Myles shook his head. "It is good that you did. I think there is more to Peggy Delwyn than thievery!"

Cutlake's eyes widened. "I don't know what you mean, sir?"

"I'm fairly sure that woman is the reason there was a body concealed in the bed," Myles said.

Cutlake had paled. "She murdered her? Good Lord! And Slouch?"

"I don't know, but I want to look in the house. I think there's a good chance he's here," Myles said, pointing towards Slouch's doorway.

"A revenant?" Cutlake sounded suddenly unsure. "One of the women said they saw him as one, raised from the ground."

"Not quite. Is there anywhere Peggy goes that she keeps to herself, anywhere you've not been?" Myles said, casting his eyes around the small workshop.

Cutlake shook his head. "There's only this workshop and the yard at the back."

"So, it's the house then," Myles said, turning his head back towards the doorway.

"It's locked, sir. Kemp still has the keys, and since they took away that unfortunate girl, it's not been opened again," Cutlake said.

"I'd lay a wager that Peggy has a key. Come on," Myles said leading the way from the workshop into the small hall, reaching down he rattled the door handle. "Locked. Can you force it?"

Cutlake moved forward, cast his eyes over the door, and put his shoulder against it. At first, the noise from the wood was slight, but a moment later, the door moved, and the sound of splintering timber met their ears as the latch tore through the frame.

"There you go, sir," Cutlake said smiling and holding the door open for Devereux.

The odour of death was still present, but nowhere near as bad as it had been. It had infused the house and provided a disturbing welcome. "Lock the outer door to the street. I don't want anyone coming in here while we are searching it," Myles instructed.

Cutlake returned a moment later. "What are we looking for, sir?"

"I'm not sure yet, something that shouldn't be here," Myles said, stepping first into the downstairs front room.

The shutters were closed, but a little light seeped through the gap in the middle, Myles flipped the latch and let them swing open. The room was empty, the furniture gone, the hearth cold and still filled with the last ashes. There were crumbs on the floor, Myles scattered them with his boot. Guessing this would have been where Slouch's chair had sat. A cleaner square on the wooden floor, with the side facing the fire darker and worn where Slouch's feet would have been. There was dust on the floor, and it was undisturbed. The fire basket was gone and the irons, but a few pieces of kindling remained and taking one Myles raked through the ashes in the fire. A grey plume rose from the hearth, but nothing was hidden beneath them.

The other room downstairs was the kitchen. Four stone steps led down to it, and again, it was empty. Myles pulled the narrow shutters open, letting light inside. Pots and pans had gone, leaving only marks on the shelves to tell where they had once sat. The room was narrow. One side had a cooking fire, the other shelves. There was nowhere to conceal anything.

Grumbling, Myles made his way up the stairs. There were two rooms; Slouch's bedroom sat directly over the front room; heat from the downstairs fire would have warmed it. The bed frame still sat lonely in the centre of the room. The dreadful mattress was thankfully gone. All that remained on the floor were a few strands from the stuffing that had been dislodged when Daytrew's men, gagging, had removed the soiled and rotting corpse. But nothing else remained.

Slouch had used the final room as an office. Myles knew this as he'd been in it when settling debts and receiving his payments from the botcher. There had been a table, two rough chairs, and a coffer against one wall. All were now gone. All that was left were marks to show where the table and coffer had once stood.

"There's nothing here," Cutlake said, coming to stand behind Myles.

"There must be! This doesn't make any sense," Myles raked his hands through his hair and turned around. "It's here, it has to be."

"What's here?" Cutlake said, throwing his hands wide. "The house is empty."

Myles paced across the office and opened the shutters. Banked behind them was a thick line of dead black flies. The house had been full of them when he'd been here before. An involuntary shudder ran down Myles' back. There was nothing here. The room was over the kitchen; it didn't have its own fireplace, and warmth would come from the cooking fires below.

Myles walked back across the office and suddenly stopped halfway across the room.

The kitchen!

That was it! The bloody kitchen was too small.

"Come on, Cutlake. It's downstairs," Myles bolted from the room, his boots hammering down the stairs. He ran down the short corridor and dropped down the stone steps into the kitchen. "We are under the room upstairs; the kitchen is too small."

Cutlake was still standing at the top of the steps, his arms folded. "I don't know what you mean, sir."

"There's another room, somewhere along here. There has to be," Myles had his hands on the wall, "Help me, man!"

There were four rough shelves. Myles grasped the edge of each. They were all firmly fixed to the wall, and nothing moved.

At the end of the run of shelves was a shorter one, maybe two feet and set halfway up the wall. Myles grasped this one. The shelf didn't move, but the wall behind flexed. Myles grinned.

"It's here!" Myles announced triumphantly, tugging again at the shelf. The wall moved slightly, but there was nothing more. Myles ducked down and looked beneath the shelf. There was a metal ring. Grasping it, Myles pulled. It didn't move. Bending down and peering beneath the shelf, he saw a thin, narrow gap to the ring's left. Myles tugged it sideways and heard the unmistakable sound of an iron bolt moving on the other side.

"We've found it, Cutlake!" Myles pulled on the shelf, and this time, it moved. It was attached to a panel, the shelf was disguising a door, and it swung open. What was on the other side made Myles step back in horror!

The corpse was fixed to a board. There was a rope across its forehead to keep the head upright, and the rest of it was pinned to the wood with long, blackened nails that protruded from the flesh. And to the corpse's right, her arms crossed and glaring at him was Peggy Delwyn.

"Good God!" Myles heard his own voice as if it were from somewhere else. "What have you done, woman?"

"Master Devereux, the deeil's spawn if ever there was one! Do you want to have one last argument with Slouch?" Peggy cackled.

"What have you done to him?" Myles said, his eyes on the mutilated body.

"It's a powerful thing, a revenant, but 'ard to create. That idiot girl's soul soured her flesh, and she putrefied. I thought Slouch would be better, but he's still filled with rot," Peggy peeled the sheet down from the corpse.

Myles' stomach turned, and his hand covered his mouth.

The corpse was split from the breastbone to the groin, and it was hollow. The flesh had sunk around the ribs, and inside the hollow cage of the man, the reddened remains of sinew and gut still clinging to the bones had begun to shrivel and dry.

"His rotting guts are gone, and we've picked his addled brains out through his nose," Peggy reached up and lifted Slouch's nose up, revealing the cavity below.

Myles paled.

"It's not easy," Peggy let the disfigured nose drop back, "They were stuck fast to his brainpan; we had to use a scraper to mash 'em and then slop them out of his nose. There over there if you want to see."

Myles' eyes followed the direction of Peggy's arm to where a bucket sat in the corner. The contents of his stomach threatened to leave again.

"But it wasn't enough," Peggy said sadly and pulled the rest of the sheet from the body. "His legs have gone bad. I stripped one of the rotten flesh, but it won't dry as it should, and I'm nearly down to the bone. Look."

Myles' eyes couldn't help themselves. The lower part of Slouch's body had fared no better than the top. The right leg was cleaved to the bone of flesh, some long sinews remained, dried and twisted, and the foot was intact and wrapped in cloth, but swollen and deformed. The left leg was bloated from the knee up over to where Slouch's genitals dangled; they at least hadn't been exposed to the treatment of Peggy's knife.

"Tis a shame. I tried, but it'll not do, not at all," Peggy said, disappointed and letting the sheet fall back. "Might be able to save 'is head. But that'll be about it, I reckon."

"Cutlake," Myles croaked, "Have you seen this abomination?"

"Aye, sir," Cutlake said, his voice a quiet whisper in the room.

"Why have you done this?" Myles gasped, his voice uneven.

"Tis a vessel for the De'vil's child," Peggy said.

Myles stared in horror at her. "How many bodies have you mutilated?"

Peggy wagged a finger at Myles. "You should know, Master Devereux, you can't start well at everything. It takes time, and I am getting better."

"The Harrington child, is that why he disappeared?" Myles asked.

Peggy pulled a face. "He swelled up like a dead dog's stomach; it was some of my fault and also owing to 'im being a child."

"And his father came looking for him, didn't he? Did you kill him as well?" Myles continued to question.

Peggy grinned. "Sent 'im to rest with 'is son, es' at the bottom of Slouch's well."

"How many have you murdered? Did you murder Slouch?" Myles asked.

"Aye. The darker the soul, the better they are," Peggy declared, "that's why that bloody girl Marnie rotted so fast. Slouch had a cold heart, but he was not Godless enough. Just look at 'im? That's why he's rotten. Left money to Kemp for masses for his soul, that's why I reckon he's gone bad. You wouldn't do anything as foolish as that would yer, Master Devereux."

"And that's why you bought naytron from Finney?" Myles said.

Peggy looked genuinely surprised. "Well now, Master Devereux, you see, you do know a thing or two about the arts of darkness, don't you? It's here," she raised a bag from the desk and shook it. This'll cure you, dries you like a winter leaf, and keeps away the rot. I used it on old Slouch, and it works. I didn't have enough, but now I do."

"That's why you were stealing from Slouch, to buy that from Finney?" Myles said.

"Who told you that?" Peggy spat.

"You left an unpaid bill, thinking it'd be forgotten about when Slouch was dead, but Finney tried to charge me for it, and as you say, I know what naytron is used for," Myles said. "It's for curing the dead."

Peggy smiled. "I always said you were a clever un'."

"Cutlake, keep her in here while I send Langston for Justice Daytrew," Myles pointed a long finger at Peggy. "You will burn for this witchery; the only shame is that there isn't a fire hot enough outside of hell for you."

Peggy shook her head. "I always said you 'ad a dark soul. An' I think it'll be just dark enough for 'im."

Myles stepped back, suddenly unsure. "What do you mean?"

She dipped her hand into her apron pocket and pulled out a small doll. It was no child's toy, the figure was of a man, neatly made, sewn with care, made no doubt from remnants from the botchers shop. It had been dyed black, apart from the face which retained a pale yellow linen colour onto which were stitched nose, mouth and eyes.

As realisation dawned, Myles' mouth went dry.

"Watch her, Cutlake; I'll listen to no more of this; I'll send for the sheriff," Myles said, his knees suddenly weak.

As he turned, he felt the woman's hands around his neck, sour breath on his face, and her nails clawing into his flesh.

"Get off me, woman!"

There followed a moment of confusion. Cutlake banged into them, the hold around his neck was broken, and Peggy retreated laughing.

Myles, gasping at the sudden pain, slapped his hand to his neck; when he drew it away, his fingers were blotched with blood. "Damn you to Hell, woman."

Peggy had pulled his poniard from the sheath and held it out, levelling it towards both men. "You think you are too clever for the likes of me, don't you?" She said.

Myles took a step back slowly, his eyes moving between the tip of the weapon and Peggy's grimly set face. "Too clever for you? Why would you think that? You are the one holding the blade?"

Peggy grinned, revealing a row of poor teeth. "You've the cunning of the Devil in yer, that's for sure but .... Just stop where yer are. Don't think I won't use this."

"Put it up. There are two of us. Take it from her, Cutlake, but don't harm her. I want her to be able to answer the justice's questions well." Myles swallowed hard, his throat dry, and an erratic pulse throbbed in his neck.

Peggy's face split and a cackle of ridiculously high-pitched laughter rattled around the room. Myles winced.

"There's going to be harm, Master Devereux," Peggy said, still laughing.

Myles blinked hard. Sweat on his forehead was beading, and he could feel it running down his temples. He raised his hand and tugged involuntarily at his collar.

"What do you mean?" Myles' voice seemed to catch in his throat.

Peggy laughed, the blade dancing in the air before her. "There'll be harm. And I'll be the one doing it."

Myles suddenly felt as if a cold hand had squeezed his heart. He looked down at the blood on his fingers, and then back to Peggy, his voice slurred, "What have you done?"

Peggy laughed, the knife dancing in the air before him. "Tis too late for yer now."

Myles took in a deep breath. "Cutlake stop her."

Myles was aware of Cutlake rushing past him, and the last noise he heard before he hit the floor was Peggy's incessant laughter.

Sam Burnell

Chapter 17

It was a tavern Fitzwarren had never thought he would revisit. The Panyer probably took its name from the French word panier, meaning bread basket, an appropriate name for such a low-quality eating and drinking house. He had lodged here with his brother after he'd rescued him from the debtor's gaol at Marshalsea.

It had been a poor tavern then, but it looked worse than he remembered. Weeds were growing from the sagging thatch, daub was leaking from between the timbers, and outside the door was a vast puddle no-one had thought to fill with stones.

Inside, the benches were sparsely populated. A couple of men sat near the fire, another was eating a meal close to the door, where a little light illuminated his table, a boy was sitting on the edge of the hearthstone cross-legged shelling peas, and a woman, a fork in her hand, was piling up the sodden reeds from the floor where a leaking roof had soaked them.

Richard smiled.

Daisy.

It was the same woman he had met years ago, but time had changed her. He remembered her hair and eyes held the same deep, shining lustre of a freshly cracked horse chestnut, perfect and holding every possible shade of brown. Her hair was streaked with the hues of autumn. And they still were, but now a little bit of winter had spread white strands in her plaits and laid tracks across her face, which was now sallow and gaunt.

The woman stopped, extracted the fork from the reeds, straightened, and was about to lift another pile when her eyes met his. Recognition lit her face, and a warm and genuine smile he remembered met him across the room. A woman's voice, a searing screech, came from a doorway in the corner. Daisy's smile fell forgotten, and she turned hastily back to turning the rushes.

"Sir, welcome. Is it ale or food we can get for you?" the woman said, rounding the benches rapidly towards him. It was another women her remembered, Saskia, a bitter wench with a cold soul.

"Neither," Richard said, his eyes on the woman. A fattened belly pressed out her apron and told of the late stages of pregnancy, and the worn body told of many that had also preceded it. "I wish to speak with Daisy."

"Speak with her, oooh, well, that's a new way of putting it," Saskia cackled.

Richard sighed, and a moment later, he had a coin in his hand. The silver glinted in the poor light from the door, and the woman's eyes were fastened upon it. "I wish to speak with Daisy, and this will, I am sure, be sufficient recompense for you to find someone else to perform her tasks today."

The Saskia's eyes flicked from the coin to Daisy and then back again. "Aye, it will."

A quick, dirty hand reached to snatch the coin. Richard was faster, he caught the woman's wrist and deposited the coin into her palm, folding her fingers over the cold metal. Walking towards Daisy, he lifted her face, smiled, and said, "It's alright. Saskia said you could come with me."

"She can't hear you," Saskia said, admiring the coin in her hand, then waving towards the other woman she said. "Ger on wi' ya."

Richard led Daisy from the tavern, her hand trapped in the crook of his arm. He turned towards her when he spoke so she could see his face. "It's been a long time. How are you faring?"

Daisy shrugged and flapped her hand in the air.

"That well! I can offer you a good meal and a warm fire," Richard said.

The brown eyes were creased with something akin to suspicion.

Richard laid his hand over hers. "There's nothing to be afraid of. Do you remember Lizbet?"

Daisy's eyes widened, and she nodded, and then concern again crawled over her face.

Richard smiled reassuringly. "She is well and still a good friend to myself and my brother."

Daisy waved her hand over Richard's head and then held them wide of his shoulders, her brow furrowed with a question. Richard knew what she meant—his brother. "He is well," Richard said.

Daisy smiled and nodded.

As they walked slowly he asked her questions about her time at Slouch's, she responded in her own way. Patiently and slowly he began to understand what it was she had seen.

Richard took Nonny's hand and raised it to his lips. Her eyes remained on the ragged woman behind him, however.

""As it a broken wing?" Nonny smiled at him and shook her head, her words heavily accented with her native French.

"You know me too well," Richard grinned. "I have promised a meal. I would be indebted to you if Nathaniel could take her to your kitchens."

A ringed finger prodded him in the chest, and laughing, Nonny said. "The Queen's coffers are not filled with sufficient to pay off your debt to me! Nathaniel, if you would."

Richard took Daisy's hand, squeezing it gently, and grinned, "Nathaniel may look like an ogre beneath a bridge, but he's a good man." Then, to Nathaniel, "She can read lips."

"I resent that!" Nathaniel said, cuffing Richard on the shoulder. "Come on, lassie. I've a hole in my belly as well; let's see if we can find something in the kitchens."

Nonny tucked her arm around Richard's, and they followed Nathaniel and Daisy a short way along the corridor before she pushed the door to her room open. The air inside was heavy with the scents of the east and a comfortable warmth from the fire. "Sit and tell me what you 'ave done this time."

Richard grinned. "Her name is Daisy; she can't, or more likely won't speak, and she cannot hear, but she can understand well enough."

Nonny raised an artfully painted eyebrow. "And do you wish me to place a bowl of milk on the floor regularly for your latest waif?"

Richard reached inside his doublet and, finding his purse, cast it on the table. "That should ensure she has food and can work in your kitchens."

Using one of the purse strings, Nonny reached forward and pulled it towards her. She hefted it in her hand and smiled. "I am sure it will. But I need to know who I 'ave under my roof."

"I have lost something, and I was hoping she may help me find it. You have nothing to fear from Daisy. She's a kindness in her and is nothing more than one of the city's unfortunates," Richard replied.

Nonny laughed, and waved a finger at Richard. “The Lord gives all babes the gift of kindness, but it is life that drives it away. It survives in very few.”

“But it does survive, and madam, especially in you,” Richard said.

“You are above flattery, and it survives in us both – do not exclude yourself,” Nonny said, wagging a finger at him

Richard sat back in the chair. “Does it? I sometimes believe kindness can become a necessity or indeed just a gaudy coat we wear when it suits us to be noticed.”

A furrow appeared on Nonny’s brow. “Do not be so harsh on yourself. Who did you wear that coat for today? It certainly wasn’t for me.” Richard let out a long breath. “My conscience probably.”

Nonny reached forward and laid a hand on his knee. “That you still have one is a miracle. You cannot have kindness without a conscience, so I think you are one of life’s lucky babes who still has God’s gift.”

Richard laughed harshly. “Madam, your confidence in me is, as ever, misplaced.”

Nonny shook her head. “I’ll not argue with you. Now, tell me what it is that you ‘ave lost.”

“Myles Devereux,” Richard said slowly.

“Oh, my word! What ‘as he done now?” Nonny asked, sounding slightly shocked.

Richard shook his head. “I suspect nothing more than letting his tongue get ahead of his brain. Have you heard anything?”

"Well, of course I 'erd about the body that was lost, and that it was 'is men who had buried it. That was the gossip of London, apparently the justice nearly buried himself when the pit collapsed as well. He 'as not been 'ere for a few weeks, 'is table 'as remained empty," Nonny said, smiling. "So how is your injured bird helping you find 'im?"

"She used to work at Slouch's botchers shop, and after he had been buried at St Bride's, she had the misfortune to see him again," Richard said.

Nonny's eyes were wide. "Good Lord! So 'is body was indeed dug up?"

"It does seem so. It is hard to know what she saw. Her fright was such that the women she worked with understood enough from her that she had seen their old Master, and they may have embellished the account to spread the tale he was stalking the streets again as a revenant. But I think what she saw lacked any animation."

Nonny rolled her eyes. "I can imagine. So what does this have to do with Devereux? Has he gone into hiding after it was alleged his men had lost the body?"

"I don't think so, Nonny. Matthew tried to prevent him from leaving the White Hart, but as you well know, Devereux does not like to be bound by the rules of others. I had harboured a hope that perhaps he may have been here, but that's not the case," Richard said thoughtfully.

"So what did she tell you? Or rather, what did you gather from her that she saw?" Nonny asked, clearly curious.

"Not a lot. She slept in the back of the botchers with two of the other women, someone came in with a lamp and left the door open to the street. She went to close it, and when she did she saw her Master standing near the door," Richard said.

"Mon dieu! Maybe he does walk again!" Nonny said, sitting forwards in the chair.

"And you believe that about as much as I do. Dead bodies do not burrow their way from their graves. Unfortunately, there are many who believe this, which does not help," Richard said dryly.

"Allow a curious soul a little speculation first before you spoil it with practicalities," Nonny scolded.

"On another occasion, when I have more time, I will indulge you. However, I need to find out where Devereux is," Richard began to rise from his chair when he stopped and sat back down again, waving his arm around her room, he said, "You have a liking for the trappings of the East."

"What is it?" Nonny said.

Richard shook his head. "Myles as an astrologica, have you ever seen one?"

Nonny shook her head. "No, but I have heard of them. An intriguing curio – why do you ask?"

"Myles has one, and it may be the reason I cannot find him," Richard said, thoughtfully, recalling the sheet of marks on Devereux's desk that had clearing been made from the wheels of the astrologica.

"Why do you think that?" Nonny asked.

"It's made of gold, it's beautiful, the best I have ever seen," Richard paused, before adding, "and it doesn't belong to him."

"Ah, he has been foolish, do you think?"

"Very possibly," Richard had risen and was running a hand along the edge of a shelf. "I see you still have Sylvesto."

"I do, but the moths have been irreverent, and they've eaten one of his ears, that's why he is turned from the light," Nonny said sadly.

Richard turned the dead cat, one ear was indeed gone. Nonny, not wanting to be parted from her beloved pet, had instead turned him into a shelf ornament. Richard stroked his hand down the back of a cat who had hated him when it had been alive, when he removed his hand several tufts of fur came away. "I don't think it's just an ear, he's provided a veritable feast for them, haven't you Sylvesto?"

"Do not mock my cat, I shall 'ave him buried with me," Nonny said wagging a finger at Richard.

"If there's anything left by then, you'll be taking a bag of dust and stuffing with you," Richard laughed.

"Just turn him back, I 'ate to see 'im without an ear. He was such a proud animal," Nonny said sadly.

"And an evil one," Richard said, angling the cat on the shelf.

"Only to you, and you know that's because you sat on him," Nonny said reprovingly.

"How was I to know the scurrilous feline was there? He blended in with your cushions," Richard said laughing.

"It might be I 'ave some news for you," Nonny said smiling.

Richard abandoned the dead cat and turned towards her, an eyebrow raised. "Indeed."

"Devereux has sent two boys here to Nathaniel for, in 'is own words, 'safe-keeping,'" Nonny replied.

"Two boys?" Richard repeated.

"One has the look of a thief and the other is a fool, and both smell like they've crawled from a midden pit," Nonny said, wrinkling her nose. "Nathaniel, he will know where they are, I'd 'ave them brought 'ere but the smell!"

Richard laughed and, turning towards the door, said. "I will go and ask him."

"Not alone!" Nonny exclaimed, and rose in a rustle of silk wafting scent across the room. "I shall not be denied a little entertainment."

Nathaniel had taken the silver groat from Rogan, fed the lads and then set them to work in the yard filling the wood store. "No point having them sat around idle, especially not that one," Nathaniel pointed to the taller of the two boys who was crowned with a leather cap that was far too big for his head, the ear flaps dangling to his shoulders.

"What's your name?" Richard asked him.

"Whose askin'," the boy said mutinously.

Nathaniel clipped him around the back of his head sending his hat flying. Stooping down to retrieve it, the boy glared at Richard.

"I am looking for your master. A friend of his, you might say," Richard replied.

The boy continued to view him with suspicion.

"Do you know where I might find Master Devereux?" Richard continued.

The boy's mouth remained closed.

"Answer when you're spoken to, while you've still a tongue in your head to do it with," Nathaniel said, clipping his hand off one of the boy's ears.

Richard held up his hand. "I am sure .... your name?"

"Rogan," he replied. The response was automatic, and his top teeth fastened themselves into his lip, regret on his face.

"Thank you. I am sure, Rogan believes he is protecting his masters interests, am I right?" Richard said, addressing the boy directly.

Rogan nodded.

"And that's as it should be, a man needs to respect his master and his wishes. But the problem is, your master has gone missing," Richard replied. "And I need to find him."

The smaller boy behind Rogan was shaking his arm and muttering something that Richard couldn't hear.

"And if, for example he was in need of help, and you knew something that could be useful, then I doubt very much he'd thank you for keeping that to yourself, would he?" Richard said, his eyes on the smaller boy.

"Shut up, Tiny," Rogan shook the other boy's hand from his arm.

Richard directed his next question towards Tiny. "You know something, don't you?"

Tiny paled, and hid behind Rogan.

"And from the look of you, someone has given you a beating recently because of it," Richard said. "What if someone wanted to do that to your Master, and you knew something that could stop it?"

"Master Devereux can look after himself," Rogan shot back, moving a little to the right and obscuring Tiny from Richard's view.

"Very loyal of you to say so, and I am sure it's true. However, he's not at the White Hart and he's not taken his men with him. He has simply disappeared, and if you know something I really think you should tell me, don't you?" Richard said.

The boy behind Rogan wailed.

Richard switched his gaze back to Rogan. “It’s your decision. But look at the facts. When has your master ever left the White Hart without his men?”

Rogan swallowed.

“Exactly. Never. So, why not tell us what you know,” Richard said.

“Tell him .... It’s Slouch, Slouch’ll have taken ‘im, and he’ll come for the rest of us next,” Tiny wailed.

“Will you shut up!” Rogan turned, roughly shoving Tiny away from him.

“This is exciting! Is Master Devereux being pursued by a Devil?” Nonny said, her face alive with delight.

Richard looked at her and shook his head. “Very well, there is news of such an .... apparition within London. Your Master would struggle, would he not to battle with the powers of evil, no matter how well prepared he is to deal with any man who crosses his path.”

Rogan seemed to consider this for a moment, and the child behind him pleaded with him again, tears running down his bruised cheeks. “Master Devereux is a match for anyone, even the Devil himself,” Rogan announced his chin jutting forward.

“Your loyalty does you credit,” Richard hadn’t finished speaking before he’d caught Rogan’s arm and pulled him towards Nathaniel. “Nathaniel, if you wouldn’t mind, I’d like a private word with the lad.”

Rogan, cursing and struggling, was lifted in Nathaniel's arms from the floor, the big man laughing. "I'd keep those teeth to yourself unless you want me to sink mine into you."

With Rogan gone, Richard turned his attention to Tiny. "He's gone, nothing bad will happen to you, I promise. But tell me, please what is it that Rogan didn't want to tell me."

Tiny, sobbing, said between gulps of air. "We dugged 'im up, Master Hill made me 'elp him. I didn't want to."

"Dug up Slouch?"

Tiny nodded.

"What did they do with him?" Richard asked.

Tiny shook his head. "I dunno. When he was uncovered Master Hill told me to disappear otherwise I'd get a hiding."

"Hill sounds like a worthy employer. Anything else?" Richard asked.

"We 'erd he'd been seen again, Master Slouch. An …." Tiny sobbed.

"And what?"

"An I'm afraid…. he'll come for me …. as I broke his eternal sleep, and Master Hill …. and maybe …. Master Devereux 'cos Hill works for 'im," Tiny managed.

"It looks like you've had a beating already," Richard said.

"I asked Master Hill if I might go to purgatory forever for what I'd done and he beat me for it," Tiny sobbed.

"This is terrible. Poor child," Nonny said, waving towards the boy, although not getting too close. "You must do something."

"Must I?" Richard said, one eyebrow slightly raised, and a half-smile on his face.

"Of course you must, for the sake of the poor boy," Nonny said, and then smiling added, "And because I wish to know very much if the streets are being stalked by a revenant. Especially now that we know that Slouch is no longer in the ground. What fun!"

"Madam!" Richard reprimanded.

Nonny smiled and leaning close to his ear. "And what safer place to be than at the Angel when evil lurks in the streets."

"You would profit from even this?" Richard laughed.

"Why not? Wouldn't you?" Nonny said haughtily.

Richard shook his head. "I am sure it will be known fairly quickly that the girls at the Angel have a tale to tell."

Nonny shrugged and smiling said. "And they will!"

"What news?" Matthew said as soon as Richard returned.

"A private word, if I may," Richard said.

Matthew took the steps at the White Hart two at a time, and Richard followed him into the outer room to Devereux's own, closing the door behind him.

"There seems truth in the rumour that Slouch was dug up," Richard said.

"Are you sure? It's more than likely they dug in the wrong place," Matthew replied tersely.

"I don't believe so. I believe the woman who saw him and I've spoke to a lad who helped Devereux's man, Hill, dig him up," Richard replied.

"Hill! Well, that puts everything in a new light? But why?" Matthew said, sounding confused.

"I don't know the answer to that, yet," Richard said, then added, "The astrologica, is it still here?"

"Asto … what?" Matthew said confused.

"You've seen it, an intricate device, wheels on the top, made of gold, in a box about this big," Richard held his hands apart.

"Oh that! I don't know, why?" Matthew said.

"I suggest you find out. We both know it didn't belong to Devereux, and I would lay a healthy wager that whoever it does belong to is more than mildly annoyed at its loss," Richard said.

"Agreed. I told him to get rid of it, smelt it and pass on the gold, but he wouldn't," Matthew pulled the door to Myles room open and Richard followed him in.

Matthew advanced towards a bookshelf at the end of the desk. The finely crafted box that housed the astrologica wasn't there. "He keeps it here, to hand. The fool likes to tinker with it. It's missing."

"Could it be anywhere else?" Richard said, casting his eyes around the room.

"It's always here," Matthew tapped a finger on the shelf, "Or on his desk if he's been using it."

"Using it? He knows how it works?" Richard said, a note of surprise in his voice.

"He's not a clue, but he keeps on winding it up and scribbling notes," Matthew said. He flipped through the papers on the desk until he found one and held it towards Richard. "Here's one of them."

Richard took the sheet, he's seen it before, when he'd searched the desk for clues, it was split into columns and each on filled with different symbols, some of them had been ringed, some underlined. A smile twitched the corner of Richard's mouth, Devereux had been trying very hard to unearth it's secrets it seemed.

"And it's missing, so you think he took it with him?" Matthew said.

"It seems likely," Richard replied pulling open the drawers in the desk. "Especially if we can't find it."

"But why? Had he taken it to someone who knows how it works? He's fascinated with it and I doubt he'd sell it," Matthew hefted the lid of a coffer up, inspected the interior, and dropped it back almost immediately. "It's not in here."

"I don't know. But it has certainly complicated the issue of his absence," Richard said, "Unless there is some connection between Slouch and the astrologica that we are as yet unaware of."

"There's none that I can think of," Matthew said. "In your absence the fool, Justice Daytrew, has been back to see if Devereux has returned."

Richard's brow furrowed. "What did you tell him?"

"The bloody truth for once. I've no idea where he is, and I would send a message as soon as he returned," Matthew grumbled.

"What did he want?" Richard asked.

"Just to ask more questions about that woman I told you about, the one found inside Slouch's bed with her innards dug out, now that those clacking women have spread the news that Slouch has risen he's right sure there are some evil doings afoot. We don't need to be associated with this, I can tell you," Matthew lamented.

"What did you mean, the woman's body was dug out? How so?" Richard said slowly, pausing in the act of examining another drawer.

"Her innards were gone, cleaned out like a pigs," Matthew said, his hand moving in the air as if he were scraping with a knife, "they found nicks in the bones they'd made while they were doing it."

Richard's face froze. "Where did you say they found her?"

"Stuffed inside Slouch's old mattress," Matthew said, then reading the look of alarm on Richard's face he said. "Why? What's wrong."

"Everything. We are going to see Slouch's shop," Richard said, now he knew why Devereux had underlined the word naytron. Into Richard's mind an image of a cat appeared. Not Amica this time, but instead Sylvesto, moth eaten and with wide staring eyes that were more human than cat-like. A long dead effigy, a companion in death.

Chapter 18

Not all of Myles's senses returned to him immediately. His first awareness was of a pain in his side from the floor on which he was laid. A hip bone complained loudly, as did a shoulder bearing his weight on the stone surface. Worse, when he tried to shift his position, he found he couldn't move. It felt like he was trapped by some cold iron hold that held his arms and legs fast.

The second sensation came from within. A sudden deep unease in his stomach, followed by saliva in his mouth, a warning that the contents of his stomach were going to leave. With his eyes shut, unable to move; the next few minutes he had no control over as his muscles contracted again and again to propel the contents of his stomach from him.

Such was the violence of the bout that some of the dreadful acid vacated via his nose, burning as it did so. The floor, which had been damp, was now sodden with vomit, and he couldn't move.

When his eyes focused, they could tell him very little, only that it was dark. His cheek was pressed against a damp floor.

The door he heard open was behind him, and he was aware only of the sound of boots on the flags and a grey light breaking through the darkness.

The footsteps stopped. A boot was planted on his shoulder, rocking his body.

Myles groaned.

"Not dead then. She'll be pleased," a disappointed voice he recognised said.

Myles tried to speak, but all that emerged was a croaking cough.

"Are you trying to say something?" The voice said again.

The boot pressed into his shoulder again, this time to force him to roll onto his back. Pain like a knife cut ran from his shoulder down his back, Myles squeezed his eyes tightly shut and wondered if he'd be able to roll onto his side by himself if he was sick again or if he were about to choke. Spasms tore through the muscles around his stomach, but thankfully, it was empty, and only a thin acid was propelled from his guts, burning his throat.

Cutlake laughed. "If London could see you now! Laid in your own sick and piss I'd doubt if you could make a mouse afeard."

Myles tried to moisten his lips with his tongue and failed.

"Have you nothing to say?" The boot toed him hard in the arm.

Myles winced and shook his head.

"I don't think you understand," Cutlake said with increasing infuriation. "She's going to gut you, you're going to die, and I am going to take your place. It shouldn't be hard. Matthew'll be looking for another, everyone knows he has no real liking for you."

Myles' dry lips managed a smile at that.

"What? How can you find that amusing?" Cutlake spat.

With what he hoped was a smile rather than a grimace on his face, Myles turned his head away from Cutlake and managed to say with an effort that hurt. "I'm tired."

"Listen to me," Cutlake growled. Cutlake's boot, this time, was planted across the side of his head, the heel digging painfully into his ear.

Myles grimaced.

"Is this because you think Davey Langston, who you left on the street, is going to save you?" Cutlake laughed. "I've sent him on a wild chase across London that'll take him so long that she'll have gutted you by the time he gets back here."

Langston. Myles closed his eyes, and the curse he made was silent. It had been a hope as fragile as a cobweb in a gale, but it had been hope nonetheless.

Cutlake leaned down, his head close to Myles'. "Don't worry, you'll not meet your end alone. I'll be there to watch."

Cutlake, whistling happily, left the room. The door remained open, and the dim light still filled the room. Myles suddenly sensed where he was. They'd not moved him far. This might have even been where he had collapsed—he couldn't remember—but he was on the kitchen floor outside of the room where Peggy had gutted Slouch.

He heard Cutlake close the door at the end of the kitchen and he was sealed in darkness again, and the concealed room door was also closed. Myles began to flex his fingers; the wrists were bound tightly together, and there was no hope of freeing them. But whatever the foul woman poisoned him with was beginning to wear off. The feeling was starting to return and with it, vicious pins and needles stabbed at his muscles.

"Come on, Devereux," he said to himself and was pleased that his voice sounded, if not normal, at least understandable.

Rolling towards the wall, and digging his heels in he managed to lever himself upright, his shoulders against the wooden wall. His feet bound together, but drawing his knees towards him, he reached down towards the knotted rope. The angle was wrong, and his shoulder slid down the wall, and once again, he was laid on the floor; the only chance was that he was now the other way around.

"You useless bastard," he cursed himself as he began levering himself back up.

Myles froze. The door opened. Cutlake's boots stopped, but the whistling continued. Myles sensed he was looking down on him, but he refused to turn his head.

"Has he come back to his senses?" It was Peggy's voice.

"Let's see," Cutlake said, laughing; a rough leather bag landed near Myles' face, and he couldn't help but recoil as he saw the long square-headed nails tumble from it.

Cutlake laughed. "Don't worry, you'll not feel a thing when we bang these through you; Peggy here is going to take your guts out first."

Cutlake put a foot onto Myles' shoulder and forced him to roll onto his back and face them both.

Peggy, her right hand filled with an assortment of knives, smiled. "We'll have a fine time, me and you." She dipped her left hand into her apron and produced a small earthenware bottle with a cloth stopper. "A quick taste of this, not too much, mind you, and you'll be able to watch me while I work."

From behind them came a sudden hammering.

"Ignore it," Peggy instructed, beginning to pull the stopper from the bottle.

The hammering, more determined, started again.

"I'll go, goodbye, Master Devereux. Sadly, it seems I shall miss your final moments," Cutlake said, laughing, and left Myles alone with Peggy.

Chapter 19

The door to the botchers shop was barred from the inside. Matthew hammered on it with his fist. “Cutlake, where the hell are you?”

Nothing.

Pulling his knife from his belt Matthew used the hilt to bray the door. “Cutlake, get your arse out here now!”

Nothing.

“Damn the man,” Matthew sheathed his knife and stepped back, preparing to kick the door, when the sound of the bar lifting from the iron rests on the other side could be heard.

“Master Matthew,” Cutlake said, his eyes switching between Matthew and Richard, who he didn’t know, blinking a little from the bright light in the street.

“Devereux, is he here?” Matthew demanded

“No sir, he’s not been here. Is there something I can help with?” Cutlake said, standing squarely in the doorway.

“When was the last time you heard from him?” Matthew said.

“Some days ago, Master Matthew, I saw him when I came to the White Hart. He’s not been here since the woman’s body was found. That was a terrible business, have they ….

"A botchers shop, you say, Matthew? Can't say I've seen the innards of one before, a bit beneath your Master isn't it?" Richard interrupted Cutlake before Matthew had a chance to reply. "I've got to see this for myself. Myles Devereux's cackling women, when we next meet at the Angel, I can tell you, I shall have the upper hand."

Richard, laughing, elbowed Matthew, and before either of the other two men could move, he'd stepped over the threshold into the small hallway, sliding past Cutlake.

"Which way? No need, I'll just follow the smell," Richard said, continuing to sound amused.

Cutlake, suddenly sounding unsure, said, "Sir, Master Devereux has left me in charge. You cannot enter there."

"I think you'll find I can step where I like, can't I Matthew?" Richard said, then added. "This door I presume?"

Matthew, frowning, nodded towards Cutlake. "Go on, follow him."

Cutlake turned and followed. "The women are working at another place today; that's why there's nobody here."

"That's a shame," Richard said, approaching a wall decorated with drying rags. "Amazing to think that these scraps have any use at all."

Matthew, in no mood for casual conversation, stalked across the workshop and pushed open the doors to the yard at the back. It was empty, stinking of piss and its only occupants several abandoned buckets. “Why are they not working here?”

“Mistress Delwyn has them working further down the brook,” Cutlake said.

Richard, abandoning his examination of the drying tatters, wandered across the yard to where the two long washing tanks sat and peered into the stream beyond it. “What’s wrong with the water here? Why take them downstream?”

Cutlake shrugged and, laughing, said. “I’ve no idea, sir. It was Mistress Delwyn who directed them there, and I’ve no idea how a woman’s mind works, or how?”

“Quite right! And indeed, does a woman possess one! That’s a question, isn’t it?” Richard said amused.

“Possess what?” Matthew said, already heading back towards the workshop.

“A mind! Fickle creatures, Cutlake, they are like sheep, and require direction. You should have gone with them, don’t you think?” Richard said.

“I’ve orders from Master Devereux to ensure his property is secure,” Cutlake said defensively.

Richard clapped him on the arm. “Good man. And the house, is that secure?”

“Yes, sir. Locked up, there’s been no one in there since the girl was found,” Cutlake said firmly.

"Hmmmm. I wonder. Master Devereux's curiosity is only ever outshone by that of his cat. I wouldn't be surprised if he'd been back here to find out what had happened to her. Are you sure he hasn't?" Richard asked, a finger tapping his chin thoughtfully.

"No, sir. No one has been in there," Cutlake said a little too quickly.

Matthew had stopped and returned to Richard's side.

"Or out of there either?" Richard asked.

"No, sir. Not since the justice's men were here, but they've left now. Once the body was removed and the inquest held I don't think Justice Daytrew thought there was much point in them being here any longer," Cutlake said.

"That's extremely interesting. How do you account, then, for the wet boot marks on the doorstep to the house just there in the hall," Richard said, his voice still conversational.

"Well ...." It took Cutlake a second before he realised he was trapped.

"Let's take a look shall we," Matthew snarled in his ear, his poniard pressed into the small of Cutlake's back before he could move.

"After you," Richard said, waving an arm towards the door.

A sharp stab in the back moved Cutlake forward, reaching the door first.

"Open it."

"I can't; it's locked, and I don't have .... Ahhhh," the tip of Matthew's blade pressed through Cutlake's doublet.

Richard, reaching past him placed a hand on the door and it swung open, the splintered wood around the lock becoming apparent.

Matthew, forced Cutlake through the door first. "Go on, in. Where is he?"

Cutlake didn't reply.

Richard opened the door to his left in to an empty room, retreating he pushed open the one to what looked like it had been a kitchen.

A voice, hoarse and strained emerged from the darkness. "An unexpected pleasure."

"Devereux?" Richard dropped down the stone steps towards the speaker.

"The very same, a hapless creature at the moment, and without your help, doubtless I shall remain so," Devereux said. "I'd stand if I could."

Richard's eyes found the younger man in the dark, hunched in the kitchen corner, as his eyes adjusted to the gloom. Devereux sat on the floor, back against the wall, trussed like a fowl before a fight, his hands and feet fastened with tight, thick hemp bands.

Richard dropped to a knee before him, shaking his head. "You've certainly annoyed someone."

"The list might be extensive, would you mind?" Myles said, his broken lips attempting a smile. "Cutlake, my man is he here?"

"He is, and enjoying the vicious end of Matthew's blade at the moment," Richard already had a knife in his hands, the taught hemp split at the touch of the sharpened edge. As the bonds fell, his hands released and parted, and Myles gasped as cramped and fatigued muscles shouted in complaint. Two swift strokes severed the hemp wrapped around his feet, and Myles was fully released.

Richard lowered himself down to observe the other man in the gloom. They'd not just bound him. Before they had, it looked as if they had beaten him. His right eye was swollen, a semi-circular cut on his forehead looked as if it had come from a boot heel, the neat black doublet was missing, and the linen shirt they'd left him with was ripped and stained. His mouth and nose had bled in a steady stream, and a dark trail of blood telling of its journey was dried on his face and shirt.

Richard, a solid hold on one arm, propped him up against the wall, and said. "I'll lift you up. It will hurt like hell, so try and complain quietly."

Devereux, stripped of his finery, was lighter than Richard expected. His body was a fine arrangement of bones and skin with little meat on them to weigh them down. Richard pulled him up more easily than he had expected, and with a little more vigour than he had planned. Devereux, on shaking legs, Richard's tight hold around his upper arm, swayed but stayed remarkably silent.

"Well done," Richard congratulated him quietly.

"Is he well?" It was Matthew's concerned voice from the doorway.

"Aye, I am," Myles called back, then he pointed with a shaking hand and whispered. "It's a false door, and behind it a woman, she is a danger."

"And you would rather she couldn't get out? Am I right?" Richard said.

"She's a witch," Myles' eyes were bright when he spoke.

"Oh well, in that case ….." Richard hauled one of the shelves from its brackets and wedged it widthways across the kitchen, holding the door shut fast. "…. Do you think that will do?"

"I bloody hope so," Myles said.

Myles, on unsteady feet swayed up the steps from the kitchen. The sword he had arrived with on his back was propped against the wall, taking it he used it as a support as he made his way into the hall and out of Slouch's house.

"Cutlake!" Myles said glaring at the man, wiping one hand across his soiled face, the other still resting heavily on the quillons of the sword.

Cutlake hadn't given up yet. "For God's sake Matthew, look at him. How can you back such a man?"

"There's a woman in there," Myles waved an arm towards the house. "She's butchered

Slouch, and God knows how many more. And you were going to have her do that to me?"

Cutlake shrugged. "I agree she is a little deranged, but it was a convenient way to get rid of you. Come on, Matthew, he's already brought so much upon himself, he's a liability to your business."

Myle's eyebrows raised. "Am I now?"

"Just look at yourself," Cutlake said, with disgust.

"He has a point," Richard smiling, chimed in unhelpfully.

Myles scowled at Fitzwarren.

Cutlake pressed on. "The justice's men are aware of his poor practices with Kemp, bribing the parish clerk, forcing Wignot to hang himself and there's even a good chance he's behind Slouch's death."

Richard turned to Myles. "This is a fairly damning liturgy."

"Aye, and it's true. All of it. And worse, he spends your money, Master Matthew, like water on his vanity," Cutlake, still restrained by Matthew, spat on the floor. "Give me a sword, let me challenge him and I'll show you what he is. Stop using that sword as a crutch and face me with it."

"Hardly a fair challenge after what you've done to him, Cutlake. The man can barely stand," Richard pointed out, then extended a hand towards Myles, "If you please, Master Devereux."

Myles shifted his hold on the sword, holding it by the scabbard just below the quillons, the hilt towards Richard. In a smooth movement, Richard withdrew the sword, revealing three feet of soiled steel.

"I see you didn't heed my advice," Richard said a look of disgust on his face as he viewed the stained blade.

"There just hasn't been time," Myles said; he'd stepped backwards and was resting against the wall of the workshop.

"Release him," Myles commanded.

Matthew pushed Cutlake away, and he stumbled forward across the workshop. "Outside, Cutlake, go on."

Cutlake, still convinced he could impress Matthew, said, "Thank you."

Matthew picked up Cutlake's sword and followed him from the workshop, with Richard behind him.

Cutlake took the sword and belt from Matthew. Rather than buckling the belt on, he removed the blade and discarded the belt and scabbard. In stark contrast to the soiled blade Richard held, it was clean and shining, and the leading edge undoubtedly sharpened.

Richard thumbed the edge of his weapon and shook his head. Holding his hand up and signalling Cutlake to wait, he swung the blade several times, and hefted it in his hand, apparently trying to get the feel of it. On one of the swings, the tip was too low and grated across the flags in the yard. Cutlake's eyes narrowed, and Myles, now propping up one of the walls in the yard, looked skyward. Matthew's arms folded solidly across his chest, his face impassive, said. "Get on with it, then."

"A moment longer, if you will," Richard said, now prescribing figures of eight in the air before him; the last stroke was fast, and when the sword swung to the extreme of the arc, it pulled from his hand and clattered to the flags. Richard grinned. "Nothing broken! The weight is not quite what I am used to."

"Are you quite sure I shouldn't take that from you," Myles said from where he watched.

Richard waved a hand dismissively towards him. "Don't worry, I've quite got the feel of it now."

Richard propped the sword against the wall, opened the clasp that held his cloak at his shoulder and unceremoniously dumped it in Myles' arms. "Hold that."

Myles scowled.

"Shall we?" Richard retrieved the sword and faced Cutlake, but made no move to engage.

Both men faced each other, eyes locked together, watching and waiting. A stillness seemed to fill the yard, the air crackling with tension, the light flashing from the two steel blades, and they readied themselves to begin the deadly dance.

Cutlake shook his head and led the fight. With lightning speed, he lunged forward, his blade slashing through the air towards Richard. But Richard deftly parried the attack, his own sword moving with precision and skill. The blades touched, the high-pitched squeal of steel on steel reverberating around the walled yard.

Cutlake, still fuelled by a burning determination to impress Matthew, fought on relentlessly. His movements were fluid, his strikes powerful and calculated. He'd been trained well. But Richard matched him blow for blow, his dark eyes gleaming with a menacing intensity, and Cutlake's blade failed time and time again to pierce his defence.

As the fight raged on, their swords weaved a mesmerising tapestry of skill and strategy. Cutlake spun, his blade whirling in a deadly arc, but Richard, anticipating the move swiftly sidestepped, avoiding the lethal strike. Cutlake, sensing that he had the advantage, launched into a series of lightning-fast thrusts, forcing Richard onto the defensive, and making him step backwards across the yard.

Cutlake grinned.

The clash of their swords echoed around the yard, their movements becoming a blur of steel and sweat. Cutlake's face was etched with a grim determination, his eyes locked in a deadly stare with Richard's. Then, with a burst of adrenaline, Cutlake unleashed a flurry of attacks, his sword slashing through the air with unmatched ferocity. Richard, however, remained poised and unyielding, his defence impenetrable. The tension peaked as Richard's blade connected with Cutlake's, the impact reverberating through their arms. In a swift and unexpected move, Cutlake seized the opportunity and attempted to disarm Richard with a quick and decisive strike, and there was shock on his face when he found instead his own blade forced back towards him, and he was stumbling unbalanced with it. For a moment, the fight halted.

"It's your fortune that I have been ..... unwell. And although it's a painful admission," Richard neatly sidestepped a thrust from Cutlake, his own blade sending the other's towards the floor forcing him to stumble forwards. "I feel that prolonging this is not in my interest."

Sweat was beading on both men's foreheads. With a speed and precision he had not yet used Richard's blade went from defensive to attack. Cutlake was forced to hold his own high to deflect the force of it, stepping backwards. Cutlake responded wildly to the next thrust towards him, his anticipation of the direction wrong, and his blade slid along Richard's, squealing as it did. The blade went on until it connected with Cutlake's wrist, the point breaking through doublet and shirt to pierce the flesh beneath. Cutlake yelped, dropped his blade, and, stepping back, caught his foot on the edge of one of the troughs and landed flat on his back.

"My win, I believe," Richard said, his breathing ragged. "The lesson is apparent."

Cutlake was glaring at him from where he lay, his left hand wrapped about the punctured right wrist. "You deceived me."

"Did I? Or did you deceive yourself. You believed Myles Devereux would be an easy challenge," Richard said. "You were wrong."

"You sought to teach me a lesson? Why?" Cutlake said, gasping through the pain.

Richard laughed, and shook his head. "Oh it was lesson, but not one for you. I am afraid, you have damned yourself beyond rememption."

Myles, surprised by Fitzwarren's words, crossed the yard and returned the cloak. Turning towards Matthew, he held his hand out. "Your blade."

Matthew handed it over. "Make sure he doesn't disappear; I'll send for the justice."

"Oh, he won't disappear," Myles said, with an evil smile.

Epilogue

It took some persuasion, and an eventual threat of physical violence from Matthew before Devereux let his retie to bonds and put him back in the kitchen. He could hear Peggy's voice from the other side of the wooden wall, and her curses damning his soul to the hottest pits of hell.

Luckily he did not have long to wait until Justice Daytrew, summoned to Slouch's house found Peggy Delwyn's next victim trussed in the kitchen and her last one nailed to a board in the concealed room.

There was a certain amount of ignominy in being rescued from the clutches of a murdering witch by Justice Daytrew and Myles bore it with as much bad grace as he could muster.

Fitzwarren had said John Dee had something similar, but not as grand. Myles pressed the diamond, opened the box, and lifted the treasure out.

It was, in terms of craftmanship, definitely the finest item he had ever owned. It was quite definitely fit for a king, or indeed a queen. Myles had made some light general enquiries about the ship Leggy Dodds had been unloading just before he stole the package, and had found out very little. It had come from Spain, and was carrying a very mixed cargo, the main part of which was wine and cloth from Spain.

So far the item had not, from anything Myles had heard, been reported as stolen. Although Myles wondered if that was for the simple reason that it was difficult to report something that Queen Mary would view as Heretical as stolen. It's very purpose made that problematic. Although Myles was not fool enough to believe that the loss would be something the owner would simply forget about. Putting a price on it was difficult, but even its base weight in gold would be a small fortune.

Amica had slid onto his knee, and Myles ran a hand over her smooth fur, her rough tongue had found his scraped knuckles.

Myles fixed a quizzical gaze on the cat. "Is that because you are feeling sorry for me, or because I taste good?"

As if in answer, Amica finished cleaning the back of his hand and lay her head on it.

A knock a the door was quickly followed by the appearance of Matthew's head around it. "Fitzwarren is here."

Myles waved a hand in the air. Matthew disappeared and a moment later Richard stepped into the room, closing the door behind him.

Richard didn't wait for an invitation, he pulled a chair towards the opposite side of the desk and seating himself pulled the astrologia across the desk. “Matthew thought this was gone.”

Myles frowned. “Why?”

“When we searched your room it wasn’t in its accustomed place,” Richard said.

Myles’ sat upright in the chair. “You did what?”

“How else were we going to find you, and it was advantageous as it happens,” Richard pushed the piece of paper before Myles. “You wrote naytron on here last, and that nearly sent me to the apothecary, Finney, but when Matthew told me the dead woman had been hollowed out and there was a purchase of naytron, then I came to the same, slightly chilling, conclusion that you did.”

“If you’d gone to Finney’s well ...” Myles shuddered.

“Indeed, it may have been too late. Somethings are best not dwelt upon,” Richard said, reaching inside his doublet he produced a small piece of parchment, changing the subject he said. “I have a gift.”

“A gift?” Myles without hesitating leaned forward and took the paper.

Richard’s eyebrows rose. “So much for the joy of anticipation.”

Myles upfolded it. Read the name and looked up again. “Who is Edward Carfax?”

“He was an agent of the crown, and was responsible for ensuring protestant writings were found, I am sorry, Myles, he is the man who helped to produce the evidence that convicted your brother," Richard said.

Myles swallowed hard, looking down at the name again, the letters swam. "Edward Carfax," his voice was a whisper.

"Indeed. Do with that as you wish," Richard said, then turning the astrologica towards him and fishing out the sheet on the desk with Myle's notes on the machine he said, "So how close have you got, do you think, to fathoming it's working?"

Myles willingly allowed himself to be steered down a new conversational path, and for the moment set aside the name and it's implications. "You can see, not very far."

"You've been a diligent student, by the looks of this," Richard tapped the sheet of paper.

"But what does it mean? There's no pattern? At least not one I can discern?" Myles said.

Richard laughed. "Does life have a pattern? If it does, I've yet to see it. And we need to go to the Angel tonight? So bedeck yourself in your tailors finest, wear as many jewels as you can carry and bare your scars like battle wounds. Matthew would like London to know that Myles Devereux fears no-one. Not even the Devil. And ...."

"And what?" Myles asked.

"You are paying," Richard, then asked. "What have you done with Cutlake?"

Myles shrugged. "What I had to do."

Richard inclined his head on one side. "Wise. A second chance is often the one that kills."

The fire started slowly. At first it didn't seem to have caught and Myles, glaring at the house began to wonder if it had taken. Suddenly, borne on a strong breeze came the scent of burning. A slight acid tang, the messenger that all was not well. Myles' eyes scanned the dark building, if there was smoke, the night was hiding it from view. Then a faint orange glow in an upper window appeared, and a moment later the screams began.

"Fire .... Fire ... fire...."

"Lord save us!"

The tavern's main door was to the right of the center of the building, and it was the only exit. The rear doors wouldn't open, wedges had been forced beneath the bottom of the door, and for good measure three firkins, were stacked against them. So the only exit was at the front. And exit they did, screaming, crying, clad in their shifts, to stand sobbing in the street as fire took hold of the building.

Myles' gaze was on the upper floor, two windows from the end. A room that was now a prison. The door wouldn't open, that too had been quietly sealed while the sleeper within snored, a little too much ale inside him to wake when there was a faint tapping beyond his room. Myles waited. He was sure the man inside would be hammering on the door, hauling on the handle, trying to pull it open. He'd have heard the warning shouts and the building would be filling with smoke, seeping its way through cracks and gaps in the wood, sneaking beneath his door to choke and terrify him.

The shutters flung open to the room. Even from this distance Myles heard them banging loudly open, and from the window Edward Carfax appeared, in his shift, terror on his face.

"Jump man, come on," it was the landlord of the tavern in the street below who'd heard Carfax's screams for help.

Carfax didn't reply immediately, his hands over his face he was coughing loudly.

Myles smiled. The smoke must be making its way through the ceiling to him and sneaking under his door.

"Come on, man, jump," the landlord shouted again.

Carfax shook his head, then screamed, his fists before him, shaking them furiously.

"Save yourself, 'tis no great distance," this time another, next to the landlord leant his persuasive shouts. "Jump, afore the fire is upon you."

Myles' horse shifted beneath him, unsettled by the smoke blowing towards them.

Myles, without taking his eyes from the window, leaned down and patted her neck. “Not long now.”

Sitting back up, he held his reins a little firmer to reassure the mare and wondered if it would be the smoke or the fire that sent Carfax to the Devil. Hopefully the latter. He’d witnessed the lick of flames on living flesh, it feasted with no heed to the pleas for mercy, it had no ears and no pity.

Myles smiled. His dark eyes hard as flint and as cold as ice at Candlemass. He too had no pity. Carfax’s screams did not unsettle him, several of his men, he noted, were averting their eyes, looking at the ground or their horses necks, distracting themselves by reassuring their mounts. Not wanting to witness the demise of the man whose piteous cries were reaching them as he shrieked and pleaded.

“Jump man, afore it is too late?”

A cart had been hastily dragged by three men from across the street, the back filled with pig manure, it bridged the gap between the ground and the window where Carfax howled for release.

“Jump, man, now.”

They stood back, their cries of encouragement ignored. Looking up in confusion as the man above them, choking in the smoke, his fists side by side shaking them as if at an angry foe. What they couldn’t see were the tight narrow chains that criss-crossed his window, nailed tightly to the frame making the window as inescapable as if it had been in a prison cell.

For a moment Carfax disappeared in a cloud of smoke. Myles frowned as his quarry was lost from view. Then the wind scooped up the smoke, wound it together and send it twisting up over, clearing the window. Carfax's pleas had turned to anguished shrieks.

Myles, sitting straight in the saddle, nudged his horse forward from the dark street where he had watched, unseen, his men following. He rode towards the blazing Inn, stopped for a moment, and smiled malevolently up at Carfax, his shift was ablaze now, and the scent that reached down to them from the window carried with it the acid edge of burning hair.

Carfax's eyes for a moment, wide, filled with pain and desperation met those of Myles Devereux below him in the street. A sob escaped from him followed by a garbled plea. Myles simply shook his head slightly and continued to watch the grisly scene. Those below knew now there was no saving the man at the window, the flames had too tight a hold upon him. A few moments later he fell forward, his right arm slipped through a gap in the chains, and snagged holding his flaming body upright.

Those in the street watched, horrified, as the hand, extending from the open window clawed the air. Devereux watched until the hand ceased, and hung motionless from the extended arm.

Justice delivered, Myles pressed his right heel gently into the mare's flank and turned her from the burning inn. He was pleased to note that despite Fitzwarren's assurances that revenge in itself delivered no earthly pleasure, he was wrong. Myles was feeling particularly satisfied with the evenings events, and his soul felt lighter for it as well.

He wasn't tired, it was something else that was keeping him from leaving his bed. A combination of comfort and happy contentment. If there was anything that needed doing it wasn't weighing on his mind, and if there was something that he should attend to he simply didn't care. Not today anyway. He usually awoke and was wrapped in a fever of energy propelling him from one task to another. But not today.

The bed was comfortable. Sumptuously so. The temperature perfect and the linen against his skin smooth and soft. From beneath his pillow the scent of lavender seeped, a delicious reminder of warm summer months, the scent of the sun. Myles breathed in deeply, his eyes closed, with little intention of vacating his bed. His left shoulder was a little warmer than the rest of him, and he didn't mind. Amica, curled up, sleeping soundly was half on his pillow and half in the bed.

All around him he could hear the noise of the White Hart. None of it was jarring on his nerves, it was just the gentle noise of life. Beneath him, deadened by the rugs that covered the boards on his floor, came the sound of laughter. Women's voices, in harmony, drifted up towards him, punctuated with an undulation of chatter. His rooms were above the kitchens, and with good reason, the bread ovens sent a heat upwards that was welcome, for most of the year. In the yard, from beyond the open shutter, came the dull uneven rumble of hogs heads on the cobbles, the noise roiling around the inside of the empty barrels. In the outer room he could hear Matthew's voice, it was loud, and he smiled, knowing that the man was raising his voice in disapproval that Myles had not risen. He didn't care.

Myles stretched his back and settled again onto the mattress, Amica, next to him, shifted her body, her arched back pressing against him.

Maybe .....

Myles opened his eyes in an instant of shocked realisation.

Maybe he was happy.

Christ!

Printed in Dunstable, United Kingdom

63495339R00170